Inferno 2025: The Future of Ca

Azhar ul Haque Sario

Copyright

Copyright © 2025 by Azhar ul Haque Sario

All rights reserved. No part of this book may be reproduced in any manner whatsoever without written permission except in the case of brief quotations embodied in critical articles and reviews.
First Printing, 2025

Azhar.sario@hotmail.co.uk

ORCID: https://orcid.org/0009-0004-8629-830X
Disclaimer: This book is free from AI use. The cover was designed in Microsoft Publisher

Contents

Copyright 2
The Pyrocene: Have We Entered the Age of Megafire? 4
Breathing Fire: The Invisible Toll on Human Health 12
The Price of Fire: Economic Impacts and the Path to Recovery 23
Building the Fire-Wise City: Reimagining the Wildland-Urban Interface 36
Learning to Live with Fire: Shifting from Suppression to Coexistence 50
Fire and Inequality: The Unequal Distribution of Risk and Resilience 61
Citizen Scientists on the Fire Lines: Harnessing Community Power for Wildfire Resilience 71
Parched Earth, Burning Forests: The Intertwined Challenges of Wildfire and Water Scarcity 87
The Lingering Haze: Unveiling the Long-Term Health Effects of Wildfire Smoke 97
Wildfire's Wake: Assessing the Ecological Impacts on California's Biodiversity 112
The Human Exodus: Decision-Making and Behavior During Wildfire Evacuations 122
Trial by Fire: Social Media's Role in Disaster Communication and Misinformation 132
The Retreat Dilemma: Ethical and Practical Considerations of Managed Relocation 147
From the Ashes: Protecting and Restoring Cultural Heritage in the Wildfire Era 159
About Author 171

The Pyrocene: Have We Entered the Age of Megafire?

Megafires: The New Breed of Wildfire

Wildfires have always been a part of nature, shaping landscapes and ecosystems. But in recent decades, a new breed of wildfire has emerged, one that defies historical norms and poses unprecedented challenges to fire management and suppression efforts. These are the megafires, blazes of extraordinary size, intensity, and destructive power that are reshaping our understanding of wildfire behavior.

What Sets Megafires Apart?

Megafires are not merely large wildfires; they represent a significant departure from historical fire regimes. They are characterized by:

Massive Scale: Megafires often burn hundreds of thousands of acres, sometimes exceeding a million acres, dwarfing the size of typical wildfires. This vast scale makes them incredibly difficult to contain and manage.
Extreme Intensity: Megafires exhibit extraordinary fire behavior, generating intense heat, towering flames, and powerful convective currents. This intense burning can create its own weather patterns, including fire-generated thunderstorms (pyrocumulonimbus clouds) that can further spread the fire through lightning and strong winds.

Unprecedented Destructive Power: Megafires cause widespread devastation, consuming vast swaths of forest, destroying homes and infrastructure, and impacting air quality over large regions. They can also have long-lasting ecological consequences, altering soil composition, disrupting water cycles, and impacting wildlife habitats.
Resistance to Control: Megafires often exhibit extreme fire behavior that makes them resistant to traditional suppression techniques. Their sheer size and intensity can overwhelm firefighting resources, rendering containment efforts ineffective.
The Role of Fire Science, Ecology, and Climate Data

Understanding the megafire phenomenon requires a multidisciplinary approach, drawing on insights from fire science, ecology, and climate data.

Fire Science: Fire scientists study the physical and chemical processes involved in combustion, fire behavior, and fire spread. Their research helps to explain the extreme fire behavior observed in megafires, such as the formation of fire whirls, long-range spotting, and the creation of pyrocumulonimbus clouds. Fire science also provides insights into the effectiveness of different fire suppression techniques and helps to develop new strategies for managing megafires.
Ecology: Ecologists study the interactions between organisms and their environment, including the role of fire in shaping ecosystems. Their research helps to understand the ecological consequences of megafires, such as the impacts on biodiversity, nutrient cycling, and water quality. Ecological studies also provide insights into the factors that contribute to megafire risk, such as fuel accumulation, changes in vegetation composition, and the presence of invasive species.
Climate Data: Climate change is a major driver of the megafire phenomenon. Rising temperatures, prolonged

droughts, and altered precipitation patterns are creating hotter, drier conditions that increase the risk of large, intense wildfires. Climate data helps to track these trends and predict future fire risk, informing fire management strategies and adaptation efforts.

Case Studies: Examples of Megafires

Several recent megafires illustrate the characteristics and impacts of this phenomenon:

The August Complex Fire (2020): This fire, the largest in California's recorded history, burned over 1 million acres, driven by strong winds and dry conditions. It generated massive pyrocumulonimbus clouds, creating its own weather patterns and spreading embers far beyond the fire front. The August Complex Fire caused widespread devastation, destroying homes, infrastructure, and critical wildlife habitats.

The Bootleg Fire (2021): This fire in Oregon burned over 400,000 acres, fueled by hot, dry conditions and strong winds. It created its own weather system, generating fire tornadoes and pyrocumulonimbus clouds that produced lightning and further spread the fire. The Bootleg Fire caused significant air quality impacts, blanketing the region in smoke and impacting air quality as far away as the East Coast.

The Dixie Fire (2021): This fire in California burned nearly 1 million acres, becoming the second-largest fire in the state's history. It was driven by extreme drought, high temperatures, and strong winds, exhibiting erratic fire behavior and challenging suppression efforts. The Dixie Fire caused extensive damage to communities, infrastructure, and natural resources.

Conclusion

Megafires represent a significant departure from historical fire regimes, posing unprecedented challenges to fire management and suppression efforts. Their massive scale, extreme intensity, and destructive power underscore the need for a deeper understanding of this phenomenon and the development of new strategies for mitigating its impacts. By integrating insights from fire science, ecology, and climate data, we can gain a more comprehensive understanding of megafires and develop more effective approaches to fire management in a changing climate.

In addition to the information provided, I would also like to add the following:

Megafires are a global phenomenon, occurring in many different ecosystems around the world.
The impacts of megafires are not limited to the immediate fire zone. They can also have far-reaching effects on air quality, water resources, and human health.
Megafires are a complex phenomenon with many contributing factors. There is no single solution to the megafire problem.
We need to adopt a holistic approach to megafire management, one that addresses the root causes of these fires and promotes ecosystem resilience.

  The year is 2025, and California is a scorched battleground. Megafires rage across the land, monstrous infernos that devour forests, homes, and lives with terrifying ease. The Mendocino Complex Fire, a beast born from faulty power lines and fueled by drought-stricken vegetation, tears through Northern California, leaving a trail of ash and heartbreak in its wake. In the south, the Thomas Fire II explodes near Ventura, driven by relentless Santa Ana winds, turning paradise into a scene from Dante's Inferno.

These are not just wildfires; they are megafires, a new breed of catastrophe that defies conventional firefighting tactics. They are fueled by a dangerous cocktail of climate change, overgrown forests, and human negligence. They are the price we pay for our disregard for the environment, a grim reminder that nature's fury is not to be trifled with.

The stories of those who lived through these infernos are harrowing. Sarah Miller, a resident of Kelseyville, watched her entire life go up in flames, the fire moving so fast that escape was a desperate scramble. Firefighter Captain Mark Johnson describes battling a firestorm, flames towering over 100 feet high, a monster they couldn't control.

The scars left by these megafires are deep and long-lasting. Over 1.5 million acres burned in the Mendocino Complex Fire, more than 5,000 homes and businesses reduced to ashes. The Thomas Fire II scorched over 500,000 acres, destroying more than 2,000 homes and businesses. The economic damage is estimated to exceed $15 billion, but the true cost is immeasurable. Lives lost, communities shattered, ecosystems ravaged – these are wounds that may never fully heal.

The megafires of 2025 are a wake-up call, a stark reminder that we are living in a new era of wildfire. We can no longer afford to ignore the threat. We must invest in prevention, preparedness, and response measures. We must protect our forests, our communities, and our future. The time for action is now, before the next megafire explodes and consumes all that we hold dear.

    The world is burning. Not in some metaphorical, slow-burn kind of way, but literally, with an intensity and scale that's hard to fathom. Forget the image of California, engulfed in flames – that's just one scene in this global pyrodrama. From the Amazon's emerald lungs to the icy Arctic, a terrifying new epoch is dawning: the Pyrocene.

Imagine Australia's "Black Summer" of 2019-2020, where koalas clung to charred trees and kangaroos hopped through apocalyptic landscapes. 46 million acres – an area larger than many countries – reduced to ash. The smoke plume, visible from space, choked the air and darkened the skies, a grim testament to the 400 million tons of CO2 unleashed into the atmosphere.

Now picture the Amazon, the planet's lifeblood, ravaged by flames. These aren't natural fires, but man-made infernos, greedily devouring the rainforest to make way for cattle ranches and soy plantations. The consequences? A devastating loss of biodiversity, a surge in carbon emissions, and a disruption of weather patterns that reach far beyond the Amazon basin.

Even the Mediterranean, that sun-drenched paradise, is feeling the heat. Ancient olive groves and picturesque villages are succumbing to flames fanned by dry winds and tinderbox conditions. Greece, Turkey, Italy – all have witnessed the fiery wrath of the Pyrocene, leaving behind a trail of devastation and displacement.

And if you think the Arctic is safe, think again. Wildfires are raging across Siberia, thawing permafrost and releasing ancient carbon deposits. It's a terrifying feedback loop: the more the Arctic burns, the warmer the planet gets, and the more the Arctic burns.

What connects these disparate events? A cocktail of climate change, human recklessness, and a profound misunderstanding of our place in the natural world. We've pumped the atmosphere full of greenhouse gases, creating a planetary tinderbox. We've encroached upon wildlands, building homes and industries in fire-prone areas. And we've disrupted ancient fire regimes, suppressing natural burns that once kept ecosystems in check.

The result? Megafires of unprecedented scale and intensity, releasing gigatons of carbon dioxide into the atmosphere, wiping out entire ecosystems, and threatening the very air we breathe. The economic costs are staggering, the human toll immeasurable.

But amidst the ashes, there's still a flicker of hope. We can choose to break this cycle of destruction. We can embrace renewable energy, restore fire-adapted ecosystems, and build more resilient communities. We can learn from Indigenous fire practices, which have sustainably managed landscapes for millennia.

The Pyrocene is a wake-up call, a stark reminder that we are not separate from nature, but inextricably linked to its fate. The choice is ours: continue down the path of destruction, or forge a new path, one where fire plays its natural role, and humans live in harmony with the planet.

The world is ablaze. Towering infernos rage across continents, consuming forests, homes, and lives. These aren't just wildfires; they're megafires, monstrous blazes exceeding 100,000 acres, fueled by human actions and a warming planet. We've entered the Pyrocene, a fiery epoch where the delicate dance between humans and fire has turned into a dangerous tango.

We've tampered with Earth's thermostat, and now we're facing the consequences. Rising temperatures have turned forests into tinderboxes, ready to ignite with the slightest spark. Our insatiable appetite for fossil fuels has created a greenhouse effect, intensifying droughts and extending fire seasons.

But it's not just climate change; our fingerprints are all over this fiery mess. We've suppressed natural fires for decades, allowing forests to become choked with flammable vegetation. We've built our homes on the edges of wilderness, blurring the lines between civilization and nature's fury. And with a flick of a cigarette or a spark from a power line, we ignite the infernos that consume our landscapes.

The consequences are devastating. Megafires leave behind a trail of destruction, scorching ecosystems, polluting the air we breathe, and displacing communities. The scars on the land run deep, and the emotional toll on those who lose their homes and loved ones is immeasurable.

But amidst the ashes, there's a glimmer of hope. We can still change our tune and learn to dance with fire in a way that benefits both humans and nature. We can embrace Indigenous knowledge, using controlled burns to rejuvenate forests and prevent megafires. We can build fire-resistant communities and create defensible spaces around our homes. And most importantly, we can ditch fossil fuels and invest in renewable energy to curb climate change.

The Pyrocene is a wake-up call, a stark reminder that we're not just passive observers in the Earth's story; we're active participants. The choices we make today will determine whether we continue to fan the flames or create a future where humans and fire coexist in harmony. The time to act is now, before the flames engulf us all.

Breathing Fire: The Invisible Toll on Human Health

The year is 2025. Wildfires rage across the globe, leaving a trail of devastation in their wake. But the destruction doesn't stop there. Massive plumes of smoke rise from the inferno, blanketing cities and towns in a thick, suffocating haze. This is not a scene from a dystopian novel; it's the reality we face.

This isn't just about scorched earth and ruined homes; it's about the air we breathe. Wildfire smoke, a toxic cocktail of gases and particulate matter, is silently invading our lungs, our bloodstreams, our very lives.

Imagine a world where stepping outside means risking your health. Where children can't play in the park, where the elderly are confined to their homes, where athletes struggle to catch their breath. This is the world we're creating.

But it's not too late to act. By understanding the science behind wildfire smoke, by tracking its movement, by educating ourselves and our communities, we can start to mitigate its devastating effects.

This is a call to action. A call for awareness, for innovation, for collaboration. We need scientists, policymakers, community leaders, and individuals to come together and find solutions.

We need to invest in air quality monitoring, in smoke forecasting, in public health education. We need to develop better masks, better filters, better ways to protect ourselves and those we love.

This is not just about surviving the next wildfire season; it's about creating a future where we can all breathe freely. A future where clean air is not a luxury, but a right.

Beyond the Burn: The Silent Thief in the Smoke

The acrid smell of wildfire smoke stings our eyes and catches in our throats, a harsh reminder of nature's fury. We cough, we wheeze, and we yearn for the clear air that once filled our lungs. But the smoke's grip extends far beyond these immediate discomforts, weaving a sinister tale of long-term health consequences that linger like a shadow long after the flames subside.

A Heart Under Siege

Imagine tiny particles, so small they're invisible to the naked eye, infiltrating your body like microscopic ninjas. These are the PM2.5s, the stealthy assassins in wildfire smoke. They slip through your lungs and into your bloodstream, wreaking havoc on your cardiovascular system.

Picture your blood vessels, once smooth and supple, becoming scarred and inflamed. Plaque builds up, narrowing the passageways and choking off the lifeblood of your heart. This is the insidious work of PM2.5, setting the stage for heart attacks, strokes, and a life tethered to medication.

The Cancer Connection

Wildfire smoke isn't just a cardiovascular threat; it's a carcinogenic cocktail. Lurking within its haze are chemicals like polycyclic aromatic hydrocarbons (PAHs), notorious for their ability to damage DNA and ignite the spark of cancer.

Think of your DNA as a delicate blueprint, guiding the growth and function of your cells. PAHs are like vandals, scribbling graffiti on this blueprint, introducing errors that can spiral into uncontrolled cell growth – the hallmark of cancer.

The lungs, the first line of defense against smoke inhalation, bear the brunt of this assault. But the damage doesn't stop there. Breast cancer, brain tumors, and other malignancies have also been linked to wildfire smoke exposure.

A Child's Burden

Children, with their developing bodies and boundless energy, are particularly vulnerable to the smoke's insidious effects. Their lungs, still immature, are like sponges, soaking up the harmful pollutants.

Picture a child's brain, a universe of burgeoning connections, under siege from the smoke's neurotoxins. Cognitive development falters, IQ scores dip, and the seeds of ADHD and autism may be sown.

Pregnant women, too, carry a heavy burden. The smoke seeps into their wombs, disrupting the delicate dance of fetal development. Preterm births, low birth weights, and a lifetime of health challenges may follow.

A Call to Action

The science is clear: wildfire smoke is a silent thief, robbing us of our health and well-being. But we are not powerless against this threat.

We must demand better air quality monitoring and public health advisories, so we can take action to protect ourselves and our loved ones. We must invest in wildfire prevention and mitigation strategies, to reduce the frequency and intensity of these blazes.

And we must continue to research the long-term health consequences of wildfire smoke, to develop effective interventions and safeguard the health of future generations.

The smoke may be a formidable foe, but we are resilient. By working together, we can break its grip and reclaim our right to breathe clean air and live healthy lives.

The 2025 wildfire season has been one of unprecedented destruction, leaving a trail of charred landscapes and shattered lives across the globe. While the physical damage is readily apparent, the invisible wounds of psychological trauma are equally devastating and far-reaching. This subtopic delves into the mental health impacts of the 2025 fires, drawing upon qualitative research, including interviews and surveys with affected individuals, to understand the profound emotional toll of wildfire loss and displacement. We will explore the range of mental health challenges faced by survivors, examine coping mechanisms employed to navigate these challenges, and discuss the critical role of support systems in fostering resilience and recovery.

The Psychological Impact of Wildfire Loss and Displacement

Wildfires are traumatic events that disrupt lives, shatter communities, and leave lasting psychological scars. The experience of witnessing homes and cherished possessions reduced to ashes, fleeing for one's life, and facing the uncertainty of displacement can trigger a cascade of mental health challenges.

Common Mental Health Challenges:

Post-Traumatic Stress Disorder (PTSD): PTSD is a common reaction to traumatic events like wildfires. Survivors may experience intrusive memories, flashbacks, nightmares, avoidance of reminders of the event, negative thoughts and feelings, and hyperarousal.
Anxiety: The fear and uncertainty associated with wildfires can lead to heightened anxiety levels. Survivors may experience generalized anxiety, panic attacks, and social anxiety.
Depression: The loss of loved ones, homes, and communities can trigger deep sadness, hopelessness, and loss of interest in activities. Survivors may experience changes in sleep and appetite, fatigue, and difficulty concentrating.
Grief and Loss: Wildfires often result in the loss of loved ones, pets, and cherished possessions. Survivors may experience intense grief, complicated grief, and survivor's guilt.
Substance Abuse: Some individuals may turn to substance abuse as a coping mechanism to numb the pain and trauma associated with wildfire loss.
Sleep Disturbances: The trauma of wildfires can disrupt sleep patterns, leading to insomnia, nightmares, and difficulty falling or staying asleep.
Qualitative Research Insights:

Interviews and surveys conducted with individuals affected by the 2025 wildfires provide valuable insights into the lived experiences of those grappling with the mental health consequences of these disasters.

A Survivor's Story: Maria, a resident of a small town in California, lost her home and all her belongings in the 2025 wildfires. She describes the experience as "surreal," recalling the panic she felt as she fled her home with only the clothes on her back. Maria now experiences nightmares, flashbacks, and intense anxiety whenever she smells smoke or sees fire. She struggles with feelings of grief, loss, and displacement, and finds it difficult to cope with the uncertainty of the future.

Survey Findings: A survey conducted by the National Institute of Mental Health (NIMH) in the aftermath of the 2025 wildfires found that over 60% of respondents reported experiencing symptoms of PTSD, anxiety, or depression. The survey also revealed that individuals who lost their homes or loved ones were at a significantly higher risk of developing mental health challenges.

Coping Mechanisms and Support Systems

In the face of such adversity, individuals affected by wildfires demonstrate remarkable resilience and employ various coping mechanisms to navigate the challenges they face.

Coping Mechanisms:

Seeking Social Support: Connecting with family, friends, and community members provides a sense of belonging and shared experience, offering emotional support and validation.

Engaging in Self-Care: Prioritizing self-care activities such as exercise, relaxation techniques, and healthy eating habits helps to manage stress and promote emotional well-being.

Seeking Professional Help: Therapy, counseling, and support groups provide a safe space to process emotions, develop coping strategies, and address mental health challenges.

Finding Meaning and Purpose: Engaging in activities that provide a sense of meaning and purpose, such as volunteering or helping others, can foster resilience and promote healing.

Connecting with Nature: Spending time in nature has been shown to have therapeutic benefits, reducing stress and promoting a sense of calm.

Support Systems:

Family and Friends: The support of loved ones provides a crucial foundation for healing and recovery.

Community Organizations: Community-based organizations offer a range of services, including mental health counseling, support groups, and financial assistance.

Government Agencies: Government agencies such as the Federal Emergency Management Agency (FEMA) and the Substance Abuse and Mental Health Services Administration (SAMHSA) provide resources and support to individuals affected by disasters.

Mental Health Professionals: Therapists, counselors, and psychiatrists offer specialized care to address the mental health challenges associated with wildfire trauma.

Case Studies:

The Resilience of a Community: The town of Paradise, California, which was devastated by the 2018 Camp Fire, provides a powerful example of community resilience. In the aftermath of the fire, residents came together to support one another, rebuild their lives, and create a stronger, more connected community.

The Power of Therapy: John, a firefighter who battled the 2025 wildfires in Colorado, experienced intense PTSD symptoms after witnessing the destruction and loss of life. Through therapy, he was able to process his trauma, develop coping mechanisms, and regain a sense of control over his life.

Conclusion:

The 2025 wildfires have left an indelible mark on the lives of countless individuals, communities, and ecosystems. The psychological trauma of wildfire loss and displacement is a significant public health concern that demands attention and resources. By understanding the mental health impacts of these disasters, supporting the development of coping mechanisms, and strengthening support systems, we can foster resilience, promote healing, and help individuals and communities rebuild their lives in the wake of these devastating events.

The Fire Next Time: When Disaster Doesn't Discriminate, But Inequality Does
The crackle of flames devouring a hillside. The acrid smell of smoke stinging your eyes, scratching at your throat. The panicked scramble for safety, a desperate race against an unforgiving inferno. Wildfires, once a seasonal threat, are now a terrifying reality for communities across the globe, fueled by a changing climate and human negligence. But while fire itself may be indiscriminate, its consequences are anything but.

This isn't just about scorched earth and lost homes; it's about the deep scars etched into the lives of those already burdened by inequality. It's about Maria, a single mother in Paradise, California, who watched her mobile home – her sanctuary, her struggle – vanish in the Camp Fire's wrath, leaving her with nothing but the clothes on her back and the lingering trauma of escape. It's about the Indigenous communities of the Pacific Northwest, their ancestral lands choked by smoke, their cultural traditions disrupted, their elders struggling to breathe the air that once nourished their ancestors.

Poverty, race, and access to healthcare – these aren't just abstract concepts; they are the fault lines that determine who survives, who recovers, and who is left behind in the ashes.

The Unequal Burn

Imagine two families facing the same wildfire. One, a wealthy family living in a gated community, receives an alert on their smartphones, jumps into their SUV packed with emergency supplies, and drives to their pre-booked hotel room, their health insurance card tucked safely in their wallet. The other, a low-income family living in a densely populated area, receives a delayed warning, scrambles to gather their belongings, and ends up crammed in a crowded shelter, their children coughing through the night, their access to medication uncertain.

This isn't a hypothetical scenario; it's the stark reality of wildfire inequity. Low-income communities often reside in areas more susceptible to fire, lack the resources to prepare or evacuate, and face a grueling uphill battle to rebuild their lives. They may live in older homes with inadequate fire protection, lack insurance to cover their losses, and struggle to access healthcare for wildfire-related illnesses.

And then there's the insidious legacy of race. BIPOC communities, often relegated to neighborhoods with higher environmental risks, face a disproportionate burden of wildfire hazards. Historical redlining, discriminatory housing policies, and economic inequality have forced them into areas with greater exposure to smoke, fewer evacuation routes, and limited access to healthcare.

The Smoke That Chokes, The System That Fails

Wildfire smoke doesn't discriminate, but its effects are magnified for those with pre-existing health conditions. Imagine a child with asthma gasping for air in a smoke-filled apartment, their inhaler empty, their parents frantic. Imagine an elderly woman with heart disease struggling to breathe, the stress of evacuation exacerbating her condition, her access to medication disrupted.

These are the faces of wildfire inequity, the human cost of a system that fails to protect its most vulnerable. Limited access to healthcare, including preventive care, treatment for chronic conditions, and mental health services, can turn a wildfire's aftermath into a protracted health crisis.

Beyond the Flames: A Call for Justice

The fight against wildfire inequity isn't just about putting out fires; it's about extinguishing the flames of injustice that burn deep within our society. It's about:

Empowering Communities: Investing in community-led preparedness initiatives, ensuring culturally appropriate resources, and providing financial assistance for vulnerable families.
Bridging the Healthcare Gap: Expanding access to affordable healthcare, addressing racial disparities in healthcare, and increasing healthcare capacity in high-risk communities.
Championing Environmental Justice: Reducing exposure to environmental hazards in vulnerable communities, tackling climate change, and promoting equitable land use planning.
Strengthening Disaster Response: Prioritizing vulnerable populations in evacuations and sheltering, offering

culturally competent support services, and addressing long-term health needs.

Forging Partnerships: Fostering collaboration between government agencies, community organizations, and healthcare providers, and engaging with tribal governments to ensure culturally sensitive solutions.

This isn't just about surviving the next wildfire; it's about building a future where everyone can thrive, regardless of their income, race, or zip code. It's about ensuring that when the flames die down, the embers of justice continue to glow, illuminating a path towards a more equitable and resilient world.

The Price of Fire: Economic Impacts and the Path to Recovery

The year is 2025. The air crackles with a heat that seems to emanate from the earth itself, a grim testament to the wildfires raging across the globe. It's not just the trees and wildlife that are burning; it's our livelihoods, our homes, and our sense of security.

Imagine a world where the familiar scent of pine needles is replaced by the acrid sting of smoke, where the vibrant colors of autumn are muted by a haze of ash, and where the chirping of birds is drowned out by the roar of flames. This is the reality we face as the 2025 wildfire season leaves its mark on the planet.

The economic toll of these fires is staggering. Homes reduced to smoldering rubble, businesses shuttered, and once-thriving communities transformed into ghost towns. The cost of rebuilding is astronomical, but how do you put a price on the memories lost, the sense of place destroyed?

The tourism industry, once a vibrant source of income, is reeling. National parks, once teeming with visitors, now stand deserted, their trails obscured by smoke and their landscapes scarred by fire. Hotels and restaurants, once bustling with activity, are now eerily quiet, their owners struggling to stay afloat.

Farmers and ranchers watch helplessly as their crops wither and their livestock perish, their livelihoods going up in smoke. The agricultural sector, the backbone of many economies, is brought to its knees, leaving a trail of devastation in its wake.

Even those seemingly removed from the immediate impact of the fires feel the ripple effects. Insurance companies grapple with record-breaking claims, their resources stretched thin. Real estate markets in fire-prone areas plummet as buyers become wary, leaving homeowners with properties they can no longer sell.

The public health system is overwhelmed as respiratory illnesses surge, hospitals overflowing with patients struggling to breathe. The mental health toll is immeasurable, as trauma and loss leave deep scars on individuals and communities.

The environmental consequences are equally dire. Forests, once the lungs of the planet, are reduced to charred remains, their ability to absorb carbon dioxide compromised. Wildlife populations dwindle as their habitats disappear, leaving a void in the ecosystem.

The 2025 wildfire season is not just an environmental disaster; it's an economic catastrophe, a stark reminder of the interconnectedness of our world. As the flames die down and the smoke clears, we are left to pick up the pieces, to rebuild our lives and our economies, and to confront the harsh reality of a changing climate.

The Earth Trembles, the Market Quivers: Unveiling the Long Shadow of Natural Disasters

Natural disasters are more than just momentary bursts of chaos; they're like a stone thrown into a pond, the ripples spreading far beyond the initial splash. We see the immediate destruction – lives lost, homes shattered, businesses drowned. But what about the echoes of that destruction, the tremors that continue to shake our foundations for years, even decades, to come? Let's delve into the hidden aftershocks, the long-term economic scars that natural disasters etch into our world.

The Ghost Town Effect: When Disaster Redraws the Map

Imagine a bustling neighborhood, vibrant with life, suddenly transformed into a ghost town. This is the stark reality for many communities in the wake of a disaster. Homes lie abandoned, businesses boarded up, the air thick with an eerie silence.

The Value Vacuum: After the dust settles, property values often plummet. Who wants to buy a house teetering on the edge of a flood zone or a business with a "condemned" sign slapped across its face? It's a vicious cycle – lower values discourage investment, stifling recovery and leaving communities trapped in a downward spiral. A study after Hurricane Katrina showed property values in some areas still hadn't recovered a decade later. Think about that – a decade of economic stagnation, a generation robbed of opportunity.

Insurance Roulette: Suddenly, insurance becomes a luxury good. Premiums skyrocket, coverage shrinks, and in the worst cases, insurers simply pack their bags and leave. It's like playing roulette with your livelihood – can you afford to gamble on the next disaster?

The Great Exodus: People vote with their feet. Faced with economic hardship, shattered communities, and the looming threat of another disaster, many simply leave. This "brain drain" siphons off the very talent and energy needed to rebuild. But it's not just about who leaves; it's about who arrives. Disaster zones can become magnets for opportunistic developers, sometimes reshaping the very identity of a community.

The Bill Comes Due: Paying the Price of Recovery

The initial damage is just the tip of the iceberg. The true cost of a natural disaster unfolds over years, a relentless drain on resources and a constant reminder of the fragility of our systems.

Rebuilding from the Rubble: Homes need to be rebuilt, businesses resurrected, infrastructure stitched back together. It's a Herculean task, often hampered by bureaucratic red tape and the sheer scale of the devastation.

The Productivity Plunge: Businesses grind to a halt, supply chains snap, and workers are left with nothing to do. This lost productivity ripples through the economy, impacting everything from local shops to global markets.

Hidden Costs, Lingering Pain: The economic toll extends far beyond the physical damage. Think about the strain on healthcare systems, the surge in mental health issues, the environmental scars that may take decades to heal. These are the hidden costs, the silent burdens that communities carry long after the headlines fade.

Case Studies: Stories Etched in Loss

Fukushima's Nuclear Nightmare: The 2011 earthquake and tsunami in Japan triggered a nuclear meltdown at the Fukushima Daiichi power plant. A decade later, many areas remain uninhabitable, property values a distant memory. It's a chilling testament to the enduring economic consequences of technological disasters intertwined with natural forces.

New Orleans, a City Transformed: Hurricane Katrina ripped through New Orleans in 2005, leaving a trail of destruction and displacement. The city's demographic landscape was forever altered, with a significant exodus of African Americans and an influx of Hispanic workers. It's a stark reminder that disasters can reshape not just the physical environment, but the very fabric of society.

The Path Forward: Building Resilience in a Turbulent World

Natural disasters are a stark reminder of our vulnerability. But they also offer an opportunity to build back better, to create communities that are not just resilient, but truly thrive in the face of adversity. This means investing in robust infrastructure, embracing sustainable practices, and fostering a culture of preparedness. It's about understanding that the true cost of a disaster isn't just measured in dollars and cents, but in the human potential lost and the opportunities squandered. By acknowledging the long shadow of natural disasters, we can begin to illuminate a path towards a more secure and equitable future.

California Burning: A Fiscal Inferno

Imagine a dragon, not of myth, but of smoke and flame, its fiery breath scorching not just California's majestic landscapes, but its financial foundations as well. This isn't fantasy, it's the reality of the Golden State's wildfire crisis, a fiscal inferno that threatens to consume the very fabric of its economy.

The Dragon's Appetite: Costs Exploding

Gone are the days when wildfires were a seasonal concern. Now, this ravenous beast feasts year-round, fueled by a climate change cocktail of intense heat and parched vegetation. Every blaze demands an army of firefighters, a fleet of equipment, and a sky filled with firefighting aircraft – a financial war chest that empties with alarming speed.

Think of it like this: California's fire agency, CAL FIRE, is locked in a perpetual arms race with the dragon. Their budget? A fire hose of taxpayer dollars, stretched thinner and thinner with each passing blaze. In 2025 alone, they're projected to spend over $4 billion just to keep the flames at bay. That's enough to build a small city, vanished in smoke.

Beyond the Flames: The Hidden Scars

But the dragon's destruction doesn't end with the last ember. Homes reduced to ash, businesses turned to cinders, roads and bridges crumbling – the cost of rebuilding is staggering. Then there's the poisoned air, the scarred landscapes, and the lingering trauma, all with their own hefty price tags.

It's like trying to heal a wound that keeps reopening, a constant drain on resources that leaves communities gasping for financial air. Federal aid helps, but it's often a band-aid on a gaping wound, leaving state and local governments scrambling to fill the void.

The Squeeze: Essential Services Wither

Imagine a community forced to choose between textbooks and fire trucks, between hospital beds and wildfire prevention programs. This is the grim reality facing California, as the dragon's insatiable hunger forces agonizing trade-offs.

Schools, hospitals, public safety – all are feeling the pinch as funds are diverted to the front lines of the firefight. It's a slow burn that erodes the very foundations of society, leaving communities vulnerable and their futures uncertain.

The Dragon's Shadow: Case Studies in Despair

Remember Paradise, the town erased from the map by the Camp Fire? Or the Santa Cruz Mountains, scarred by the CZU Lightning Complex? These aren't just names on a map; they're stark reminders of the dragon's devastating power, both physically and fiscally.

Billions of dollars in damages, livelihoods shattered, the long shadow of trauma – these are the legacies of California's wildfire crisis. Each fire a grim warning, a call to action before more communities are consumed.

Facing the Inferno: A Call for Courage

California stands at a crossroads. Continue to battle the dragon blaze by blaze, or find a way to tame the beast itself? The answer lies in a multi-pronged attack:

Starving the Dragon: Invest in wildfire prevention, from forest management to community preparedness.
Building Resilience: Strengthen infrastructure, create fire-adapted communities, and support those impacted by fires.
Securing Resources: Demand increased federal support and explore innovative funding mechanisms.
The task is daunting, but the stakes are too high to ignore. California's future, its very soul, hangs in the balance. It's time to summon the courage, the innovation, and the collective will to confront this fiscal inferno and forge a path toward a more resilient, fire-safe future.

Rebuilding with Resilience: Rising from the Ashes

Imagine a community, nestled amidst a breathtaking landscape of towering pines and crystal-clear streams. Life unfolds at nature's pace, until one day, the wind shifts, carrying the acrid scent of smoke. A wildfire erupts, transforming the familiar landscape into a raging inferno. Homes are reduced to ash, businesses crumble, and lives are forever altered. This is the devastating reality of wildfires in the 21st century, a reality intensified by our changing climate.

But amidst the ashes, there's a spark of hope. A spirit of resilience ignites, fueled by a determination to not just rebuild, but to rise stronger than before. This is the essence of a fire-adapted economy – an economy that not only withstands the flames but thrives in their presence.

The Scars of the Inferno: Understanding the Economic Impact

Before we embark on the journey of recovery and adaptation, we must first understand the deep wounds inflicted by wildfires. These wounds extend far beyond the charred remains of homes and businesses:

The Immediate Toll: The flames devour not just structures, but livelihoods. Businesses shutter, jobs vanish, and the lifeblood of the community – its economy – hemorrhages. The 2023 California wildfire season alone left a gaping $50 billion hole, a stark reminder of the immediate financial devastation.

The Hidden Scars: Like phantom pain, the indirect costs linger long after the flames subside. Businesses struggle to reopen, tourism dwindles as smoke chokes the air, and the emotional toll weighs heavy on the community's soul.

The Long Shadow: Wildfires leave a legacy that stretches far beyond the initial devastation. Soil erosion, contaminated water, and ravaged habitats cast a long shadow on industries like agriculture, forestry, and fisheries, hindering their ability to flourish.

These economic consequences hit vulnerable communities and small businesses the hardest, leaving them grappling with the monumental task of rebuilding their lives and livelihoods.

Fanning the Flames of Recovery: Innovative Financing Mechanisms

Traditional disaster relief, often bogged down by bureaucracy and delays, simply can't keep pace with the urgent needs of fire-ravaged communities. We need innovative solutions, like financial firefighters, to douse the flames of economic hardship:

Catastrophe Bonds: Sharing the Risk, Reaping the Rewards: Imagine a financial safety net woven by investors who believe in a community's resilience. Catastrophe bonds are like insurance policies for disasters, providing immediate funds when wildfires strike. Investors receive interest, but if a major fire occurs, they share the risk, ensuring that communities have the resources to rebuild.

Example: In 2024, California took a bold step, issuing $2 billion in catastrophe bonds. When wildfires raged in the north, these bonds provided a lifeline, ensuring that funds were readily available for immediate response and recovery.

Community Disaster Funds: Neighbors Helping Neighbors: Picture a community chest, filled with contributions from individuals, businesses, and philanthropists, ready to provide grants and loans to those in need. Community disaster funds empower communities to take control of their recovery, fostering a sense of collective responsibility and resilience.

Case Study: The Community Foundation of the North Bay, a beacon of hope after the 2017 wildfires, has distributed millions in grants, prioritizing vulnerable populations and investing in long-term recovery.

Insurance-linked Securities (ILS): Tapping into the Power of the Market: Think of ILS as a bridge between the insurance industry and the capital markets, allowing insurers to share wildfire risk with investors. This makes insurance more affordable and accessible in fire-prone areas, providing a crucial safety net for homeowners and businesses.

Example: In 2025, a group of insurers joined forces with a reinsurer to issue $500 million in wildfire ILS, expanding coverage in high-risk areas while mitigating their own financial exposure.

Public-Private Partnerships (PPPs): Uniting for a Common Cause: Imagine a collaboration between governments and private companies, pooling their resources and expertise to rebuild and protect communities. PPPs can leverage private sector innovation and capital to develop wildfire risk assessment tools, implement mitigation projects, and foster economic recovery.

Case Study: Boulder, Colorado, partnered with a private company to create a wildfire risk assessment tool, empowering homeowners and businesses to understand their risk and take proactive measures.

Sowing the Seeds of Resilience: Green Infrastructure Investments

Investing in green infrastructure is like planting a forest of resilience, one that not only withstands wildfires but also provides a multitude of benefits. These nature-based solutions are the foundation of a fire-adapted economy:

Forest Management: Working with Nature, Not Against It: Imagine forests managed with a gentle touch, where thinning, prescribed burns, and reforestation mimic natural processes, reducing fuel loads and creating healthier, more resilient ecosystems.

Example: The Yurok Tribe in Northern California, drawing on generations of traditional knowledge and modern science, has implemented a forest management program that protects their ancestral lands and creates economic opportunities.
Watershed Restoration: Healing the Land, Protecting the Community: Picture healthy watersheds, where restored meadows and stabilized streambanks act as natural firebreaks, protecting communities from the encroaching flames.

Case Study: The Sierra Nevada Conservancy has invested millions in watershed restoration, enhancing wildfire resilience, improving water quality, and supporting local economies.
Fire-Resistant Landscaping: Creating a Protective Embrace: Envision homes and businesses surrounded by a tapestry of fire-resistant plants, creating defensible spaces that offer a buffer against approaching wildfires.

Example: San Diego incentivizes fire-resistant landscaping, transforming neighborhoods into beautiful, fire-wise havens.
Community Wildfire Protection Plans (CWPPs): A Shared Vision for Resilience: Imagine communities coming

together, forging a shared vision for wildfire preparedness and mitigation. CWPPs empower communities to identify risks, prioritize projects, and build a fire-adapted future.

Case Study: Paradise, California, rising from the ashes of the devastating Camp Fire, has developed a CWPP that guides its rebuilding efforts and fosters a culture of resilience.
Branching Out: Economic Diversification in Fire-Prone Regions

Relying solely on industries vulnerable to wildfires is like building a house on a foundation of sand. Economic diversification is key to creating resilient communities that can weather the storms:

Promoting Innovation and Technology: Sparking New Industries: Imagine a hub of innovation, where entrepreneurs and researchers develop cutting-edge technologies to mitigate wildfire risk, creating new industries and job opportunities.

Example: Flagstaff, Arizona, fosters a thriving tech scene with its incubator for wildfire-focused startups, diversifying its economy and attracting talent.
Developing Value-added Industries: From Raw Materials to Finished Products: Picture a community that transforms its natural resources into high-value products, reducing reliance on raw material extraction and creating a more sustainable economic base.

Case Study: Quincy, California, boasts a thriving wood products industry, utilizing sustainably harvested timber to create jobs and reduce wildfire risk.
Investing in Renewable Energy: Harnessing the Power of Nature: Envision a landscape dotted with solar panels and wind turbines, generating clean energy that reduces

greenhouse gas emissions and lessens the threat of wildfires.

Example: New Mexico's investment in solar energy has created thousands of jobs, reduced its carbon footprint, and bolstered its wildfire resilience.
Supporting Eco-tourism and Outdoor Recreation: Experiencing Nature Responsibly: Imagine a community that embraces eco-tourism, attracting visitors who appreciate the natural beauty while contributing to its preservation.

Case Study: Moab, Utah, has become a mecca for eco-tourism, diversifying its economy and promoting environmental stewardship.
Rising from the Ashes: A Fire-Adapted Future

Rebuilding with resilience is not just about bricks and mortar; it's about fostering a spirit of adaptation, innovation, and community. By embracing these strategies, we can create a fire-adapted economy that not only survives but thrives in the face of adversity.

This is a future where communities and nature coexist in harmony, where economies are diversified and resilient, and where the flames of wildfires, while a natural part of the ecosystem, no longer threaten our livelihoods and our way of life. This is the promise of a fire-adapted economy – a promise of renewal, resilience, and a brighter future for all.

Is Your Home Ready to Face the Flames? The 2025 Wildfire Stress Test

Imagine a world where wildfires rage with unprecedented ferocity, fueled by a changing climate and encroaching development. This isn't a scene from a dystopian novel; it's the reality we face in 2025. As the lines between wilderness and urban sprawl blur, the Wildland-Urban Interface (WUI) has become a battleground where homes and nature clash.

This year, we're putting our defenses to the ultimate test: the 2025 Wildfire Stress Test. Think of it as a fire drill for the entire WUI, where we examine the strength of our building codes, zoning regulations, and land-use planning against the growing inferno of wildfire risk.

Building Codes: Your Home's Suit of Armor

Building codes are the frontline warriors in this battle, the knights in shining armor protecting our homes. They dictate the materials we use, the way we design our houses, and even how we landscape our yards. Think of them as the blueprints for a fire-resistant fortress.

Ignition Resistance: No more tinderbox roofs! We're talking about fire-resistant materials that can withstand the onslaught of embers and flames. Imagine roofs that shrug off burning debris, walls that stand strong against the heat, and windows that don't shatter under pressure.

Defensible Space: Picture a moat around your castle, but instead of water, it's a carefully manicured buffer zone. Defensible space means clearing vegetation and reducing fuel loads, creating a safe haven around your home.

Ember and Flame Intrusion: Sneaky embers can infiltrate even the smallest cracks, igniting a fire from within. Ember-resistant vents and screens act like shields, preventing these fiery invaders from breaching your defenses.

Water Supply and Access: When the firestorm hits, firefighters need the tools to fight back. Adequate water supply and access are crucial, ensuring that our heroes have the resources they need to defend our homes.

But even the strongest armor has its weaknesses. Challenges remain in enforcing these codes, retrofitting older homes, and keeping up with the ever-evolving nature of wildfire.

California: A Trailblazer in the Firefight

California, a state all too familiar with the wrath of wildfires, has been leading the charge in building code innovation. Their stringent requirements for fire-resistant construction, defensible space, and ember intrusion protection are a model for the nation. But even the Golden State faces an uphill battle in ensuring compliance, especially for older homes.

Zoning Regulations: Shaping the Landscape of Safety

Zoning regulations are the architects of our communities, determining where we build and how we live in the WUI. They can be powerful tools for mitigating wildfire risk:

Limiting Development in High-Risk Areas: Why build a house on a tinderbox? Zoning can steer development away from high-hazard zones, preventing disaster before it strikes.

Cluster Development: Imagine neighborhoods nestled together in lower-risk areas, surrounded by a sea of open space. Clustered development reduces the overall footprint of human presence and creates natural fire breaks.

Fire-Resistant Landscaping: Forget the manicured lawns; fire-resistant landscaping is the new trend. Zoning can encourage the use of plants that are less likely to fuel the flames.

Access for Firefighting: When every second counts, firefighters need clear access to reach the fire. Zoning can ensure wide roads and adequate turnarounds for emergency vehicles.

However, navigating the political landscape of zoning can be tricky. Balancing development interests with wildfire safety is a delicate dance, and addressing existing development patterns can be a thorny issue.

Boulder County, Colorado: A Community United Against Fire

Boulder County, Colorado, stands as a testament to the power of comprehensive wildfire mitigation. Their strong zoning regulations, coupled with robust community engagement and wildfire mitigation programs, demonstrate a proactive approach to safeguarding their community.

Land-Use Planning: The Big Picture

Land-use planning takes a holistic view of wildfire risk, considering everything from vegetation management and infrastructure development to community engagement and climate change adaptation. It's about creating a resilient landscape where humans and nature can coexist.

The Tahoe Regional Planning Agency: Guardians of a National Treasure

The Tahoe Regional Planning Agency (TRPA) has taken a bold stance in protecting the iconic Lake Tahoe Basin. Their environmental thresholds, including those related to wildfire risk, guide land-use planning decisions and ensure the preservation of this natural wonder.

The 2025 Stress Test: A Call to Action

The 2025 Stress Test is a wake-up call. Wildfire risk is not a distant threat; it's a clear and present danger. We must strengthen our building codes, modernize our zoning regulations, and embrace a holistic approach to land-use planning.

The future of our communities depends on it. Let's work together to build a more fire-resilient world, where homes and nature can thrive in harmony.

Embracing the Flames: A New Era of Fire-Resilient Communities

The rising tide of wildfires, fueled by a changing climate, demands a radical shift in how we design, build, and nurture our communities in the Wildland-Urban Interface (WUI). We can no longer merely react to fire; we must proactively embrace it as a force of nature and adapt our way of life accordingly. This means reimagining our homes, our landscapes, and our very communities to coexist with fire, not fear it.

I. Architectural Alchemy: Transforming Homes into Fire-Resistant Havens

Imagine homes that stand defiant in the face of raging flames, like resilient phoenixes rising from the ashes. This vision is becoming a reality as architects pioneer innovative designs and materials that prioritize fire resistance without sacrificing aesthetics.

The Rise of Non-Combustible Materials: Traditional building materials like wood, with their warm appeal, are unfortunately fire's best friend. The future lies in embracing alternatives:

Concrete: This stalwart material, with its impressive strength and fire resistance, is being further enhanced with innovations like fiber reinforcement. Imagine sleek, modern homes sculpted from this adaptable material, standing strong against the flames.
Steel: While steel itself doesn't burn, intense heat can weaken it. Architects are countering this by encasing steel in protective layers like gypsum board or applying fire-resistant coatings, creating a shield against fire's wrath.
Masonry: The timeless elegance of brick, stone, and concrete blocks offers inherent fire resistance, adding a touch of classic beauty to fire-resilient structures.
Insulated Concrete Forms (ICFs): These ingenious forms, composed of interlocking foam blocks filled with concrete, create a fortress-like wall system that not only resists fire but also boasts energy efficiency and sound insulation.
Cladding and Roofing: The First Line of Defense: A building's exterior is its armor against wildfire. Choosing ignition-resistant materials is paramount:

Metal Roofing: Sleek and durable, standing seam metal roofs deflect intense heat and embers, offering a modern aesthetic and long-lasting protection.

Fiber Cement Siding: This versatile siding mimics the look of wood while providing excellent fire resistance and requiring minimal maintenance.
Stucco: A time-honored cladding, stucco offers a textured, fire-resistant finish that can be customized to complement any architectural style.
Clay or Concrete Tile Roofing: Evoking a sense of timeless elegance, these materials are inherently fire-resistant and provide a classic, aesthetically pleasing look.
Design Features for a Fire-Safe Haven:

Defensible Space: Creating a buffer zone around a structure is crucial. Imagine a home surrounded by a carefully orchestrated landscape, designed to disrupt fire's path:

Zone 1 (0-5 feet): A fortress of non-combustibility, this zone features hardscaping like gravel, rock, or pavers, creating a fire-resistant barrier.
Zone 2 (5-30 feet): Here, vegetation is strategically thinned and spaced, reducing fuel for the fire and slowing its advance.
Zone 3 (30-100 feet): A fuel break zone, where trees are thinned and ladder fuels removed, disrupting fire's ability to climb and spread.
Ember-Resistant Construction: Embers, carried by the wind, can ignite homes far from the fire's origin. Architects are combating this with:

Fine mesh screens: These act as invisible shields, covering vents and openings to prevent embers from infiltrating the home.
Sealed attic and crawl spaces: These vulnerable areas are meticulously sealed to prevent ember accumulation.
Non-combustible decks and fences: Composite decking, metal, or concrete create fire-resistant outdoor spaces.

Fire-Resistant Windows: Windows, often a weak point, are fortified with:

Tempered glass: This robust glass resists heat and breakage, providing a barrier against flames.
Double-paned windows with wider gaps: Increased air space enhances insulation and slows heat transfer.
Fire-rated windows: These specialized windows withstand fire for a designated period, offering precious time for evacuation.
Simplified Roof Forms: Clean, simple rooflines minimize ember collection points, reducing the risk of ignition.

II. Landscaping for Resilience: Creating a Fire-Wise Oasis

Imagine a landscape that not only enhances a home's beauty but also acts as a fire-resistant shield. This is the power of fire-wise landscaping.

Defensible Space Revisited:

Zone 1 (0-5 feet): Hardscaping dominates, with non-combustible materials creating a fire-resistant perimeter. If plants are used, they are low-growing, high-moisture varieties like succulents and groundcovers.
Zone 2 (5-30 feet): Vegetation is carefully selected and spaced, with an emphasis on low-flammability species and vertical separation to prevent fire from climbing.
Zone 3 (30-100 feet): Fuel reduction is key, with thinning and the creation of fire breaks to disrupt fire's path.
Fire-Resistant Landscaping Principles:

Plant Selection: Low flammability, high moisture content, and open branching habits are favored. Deciduous trees, which lose their leaves, are often preferred over evergreens. Native plants, adapted to local fire regimes, are also excellent choices.

Plant Placement: Plants are strategically grouped based on flammability, and flammable vegetation is kept away from windows. Topography is considered, with more fire-resistant species planted on slopes where fire travels faster.
Maintenance Practices: Regular irrigation, pruning, and the use of non-combustible mulch are essential to maintain a fire-wise landscape.
III. Community Collaboration: Building a Fire-Resilient Future Together

Imagine a community where everyone, from planners and developers to policymakers and residents, works together to create a fire-safe environment. This shared responsibility is the foundation of fire-resilient communities.

Land Use Planning and Zoning:

Restricting Development in High-Risk Areas: Development is limited or prohibited in areas prone to wildfire, such as steep slopes and canyons.
Cluster Development: Concentrating development in lower-risk areas minimizes the community's footprint in the WUI.
Creating Fire Breaks: Parks, open spaces, and greenbelts act as natural fire breaks, disrupting fuel continuity.
Infrastructure and Utilities:

Fire-Resistant Roads and Access: Well-maintained roads and adequate access for emergency vehicles are crucial. Fire-resistant materials are used for road construction and signage.
Water Supply and Fire Hydrants: A reliable water supply and strategically placed fire hydrants are essential for firefighting efforts.
Underground Utilities: Burying power lines reduces the risk of fire ignition and damage.

Community Education and Engagement:

Firewise Communities Program: This program empowers homeowners to take proactive steps to reduce their wildfire risk.
Public Education Campaigns: Raising awareness about wildfire risk and prevention strategies is crucial.
Community Wildfire Protection Plans (CWPPs): These plans identify and prioritize wildfire mitigation activities at the community level.
Building Codes and Regulations:

Wildland-Urban Interface Codes: Strict building codes address fire-resistant construction, defensible space, and ember intrusion.
Regular Inspections: Inspections ensure compliance with codes and regulations.
Looking Ahead: A Future Forged in Fire and Innovation

The journey towards fire-resilient communities is an ongoing one, fueled by innovation and collaboration. Emerging technologies offer exciting possibilities:

Advanced fire modeling and simulation: These tools help predict fire behavior and design more resilient communities.
Remote sensing and early warning systems: Early detection of wildfires enables faster response and evacuation.
Smart home technologies: Integrated fire detection and suppression systems provide real-time monitoring and automated responses.
By embracing these advancements and fostering a sense of shared responsibility, we can create communities that not only survive wildfire but thrive in its presence. The future is not about conquering fire, but about coexisting with it, respecting its power while harnessing our ingenuity to build a safer, more resilient world.

Beyond Bricks and Mortar: Embracing the Human Element in Wildfire Resilience

Wildfires are a fierce dance between nature and humans, a blazing tango where our actions and choices intertwine with the fury of the flames. In the wildland-urban interface (WUI), where homes nestle among the trees, this dance becomes a delicate balancing act. We can't simply build walls and trim branches; we need to weave a tapestry of resilience that embraces the human spirit alongside the ecological reality.

The Human Spark in the Wildfire Inferno

Imagine a community nestled in the woods. One neighbor diligently clears brush, while another leaves piles of firewood stacked against the house. A carelessly tossed cigarette, a spark from a lawnmower – suddenly, the dance turns dangerous. Wildfires aren't just about dry grass and hot winds; they're about the choices we make, the risks we take, and the connections we forge.

Community: The Heartbeat of Wildfire Defense

Resilience isn't built in isolation. It's forged in the conversations at the local coffee shop, the shared laughter at a neighborhood barbecue, the helping hands clearing debris after a storm. When neighbors know each other, they look out for each other. They become the eyes and ears on the ground, spotting hazards, sharing information, and working together to protect their shared haven.

Igniting the Flame of Knowledge

Knowledge is power, especially when it comes to fire. We need to equip people with the tools to understand the wildfire threat, not just fear it. Imagine workshops where residents learn how flames slither through the landscape, how embers can leapfrog across neighborhoods, and how even a small act of prevention can make a world of difference.

Building a Fire-Wise Mindset

Fire-wise isn't just about defensible space; it's a way of life. It's about choosing fire-resistant plants, cleaning out gutters, and having an escape plan ready. It's about teaching kids the dangers of playing with matches and encouraging responsible campfire practices. It's about creating a culture where everyone understands their role in keeping the community safe.

From "Me" to "We": The Power of Collective Action

Wildfire resilience isn't a solo act; it's a symphony of cooperation. Picture a community where the garden club plants fire-wise gardens, the neighborhood watch helps elderly residents prepare their homes, and the local hardware store offers discounts on fire-resistant materials. This is the power of collective action, where everyone plays a part in creating a safer, more resilient future.

Embracing the Future: Innovation and Adaptation

The fight against wildfires is an ongoing evolution. Drones with infrared cameras can scan for hotspots, apps can send real-time alerts, and scientists are developing new fire-resistant building materials. We need to embrace these innovations, weaving them into our strategies and adapting to the changing realities of a warming world.

A Tapestry of Resilience

Wildfire resilience is a tapestry woven from many threads: community engagement, education, fire-wise practices, collective action, and a willingness to adapt. By embracing the human element alongside the ecological, we can create communities that not only survive wildfires but thrive in their aftermath. It's a vision where the flames, while a force of nature, are met with the strength and wisdom of a united community.

Learning to Live with Fire: Shifting from Suppression to Coexistence

A Century of Suppression: Examining the History and Legacy of Wildfire Control in California

A Fiery History: How California's Battle with Wildfires Shaped its Landscape and Future

For over a century, California has wrestled with the untamable force of wildfires. These blazes, once a natural part of the state's ecosystems, have morphed into destructive infernos, leaving a trail of devastation in their wake. This complex relationship with fire is deeply intertwined with the long-held policy of fire suppression, a practice that has profoundly shaped California's landscape and its approach to wildfire management.

From Coexistence to Conquest: The Rise of Fire Suppression

Before European colonization, California's indigenous tribes held a profound understanding of fire's role in the ecosystem. They practiced cultural burning, a harmonious dance with the flames that nurtured biodiversity and fostered a healthy, balanced landscape. However, the arrival of colonizers brought a new perspective—one that viewed fire as an enemy to be vanquished. This marked the beginning of a century-long battle against wildfires, a battle that has had far-reaching consequences.

The 20th Century: A Century of Control and Unintended Consequences

The devastating fires of 1910 solidified the perception of fire as a destructive force, leading to the establishment of agencies like the U.S. Forest Service and the aggressive pursuit of fire suppression. Fire lookout towers dotted the landscape, aerial firefighting techniques were developed, and the "10 a.m. policy" became the mantra of fire management.

While successful in reducing the number of fires in the short term, this approach had unforeseen ecological repercussions. Decades of fire suppression allowed fuels to accumulate, creating a tinderbox ready to ignite. The delicate balance of natural fire regimes was disrupted, paving the way for the megafires that plague California today.

The Era of Megafires: A Reckoning with the Past

In recent decades, California has witnessed a dramatic surge in the frequency and intensity of wildfires. These megafires, fueled by decades of accumulated fuels and exacerbated by climate change, have wreaked havoc on communities and ecosystems alike. The 2018 Camp Fire, a tragic inferno that razed the town of Paradise, serves as a stark reminder of the devastating consequences of fire suppression.

Rethinking Fire Management: Embracing a New Paradigm

The era of megafires has forced a reevaluation of traditional fire suppression policies. There is a growing recognition that fire is not the enemy but an integral part of the ecosystem. A paradigm shift is underway, moving away from fire exclusion towards a more holistic approach that embraces fire's role in maintaining healthy landscapes.

This new approach emphasizes proactive fuel management strategies, including prescribed burning and mechanical thinning. It also recognizes the importance of community engagement and collaboration in fire management. Initiatives like the Yurok Tribe's revitalization of cultural burning practices and the rise of Fire Adapted Communities exemplify this shift towards a more sustainable and resilient approach.

Conclusion: Forging a New Path Forward

The history of wildfire control in California is a testament to the complex relationship between humans and nature. The legacy of fire suppression has shaped the state's landscape and its approach to wildfire management, but it has also taught valuable lessons.

By learning from the past and embracing innovative solutions, California can forge a new path forward, one that prioritizes ecological resilience, community safety, and sustainable land stewardship. The journey ahead will require a collective effort, but by working together, California can reclaim its fiery heritage and create a future where fire is not a foe but a force for good.

The Dance of Destruction and Creation: Embracing Fire's Role in Nature's Tapestry

For eons, we humans have waged war against wildfire, viewing it as a malevolent force to be subdued. Our relentless pursuit of fire suppression has, ironically, disrupted the delicate balance of many ecosystems. It's time to shift our perspective and recognize fire not just as a destroyer, but as a vital choreographer in the intricate dance of life.

Fire: Nature's Artist

Imagine a painter's canvas. Fire is the brush, its strokes bold and transformative. It sweeps across landscapes, leaving behind a mosaic of renewal and rebirth. While some may see only destruction, a closer look reveals a masterpiece in the making.

Think of the lodgepole pine, its cones stubbornly sealed until fire's kiss releases the seeds within. Or the majestic sequoia, its thick bark a shield forged in the fires of centuries past. These are but a few examples of nature's resilience, shaped by fire's touch.

A Symphony of Benefits

Fire's benefits are as diverse as the ecosystems it touches:

Biodiversity's Maestro: Fire conducts a symphony of life, creating a mosaic of habitats that cater to a diverse cast of species. From the fire-loving wildflowers to the majestic birds of prey, each plays a vital role in the ecological orchestra.
Forest's Phoenix: Like a phoenix rising from the ashes, fire clears away the old, making way for the new. It nourishes the soil, awakens dormant seeds, and sets the stage for a vibrant forest rebirth.
Nature's Cleanser: Fire is nature's sterilizing agent, keeping insect pests and diseases in check. It's a natural sanitation worker, ensuring the health and vitality of the ecosystem.
Wildlife's Architect: Fire sculpts landscapes, creating open meadows that attract grazing herds and dense thickets that shelter shy creatures. It's a master architect, designing homes for countless species.
Fire's Role in the Circle of Life

Fire is not merely an agent of destruction; it's a key player in the grand cycle of life and death. It unlocks nutrients trapped in dead plants, returning them to the soil to fuel new growth. It's the ultimate recycler, ensuring the continuity of life.

A Call for Harmony

Our relationship with fire needs to evolve. We must learn to coexist with this powerful force, embracing its role in the natural world. This means adopting fire management strategies that mimic nature's rhythms, using prescribed burns and allowing wildfires to play their ecological role where appropriate.

Lessons from the Land

Yellowstone's Resurrection: The 1988 Yellowstone fires, initially seen as a catastrophe, ultimately revealed nature's resilience. From the ashes emerged a rejuvenated landscape, teeming with new life.
Australia's Fiery Crucible: The recent bushfires in Australia serve as a stark reminder of the consequences of disrupting fire's natural cycle. It's a call to action, urging us to find a balance between human needs and ecological imperatives.
Embracing the Dance

Fire is a force of nature, a powerful and essential element in the tapestry of life. It's time to shed our fear and embrace fire's role in the dance of destruction and creation. By understanding and respecting its power, we can ensure the health and resilience of our planet for generations to come.

  Embracing the Dance of Fire: A Rebirth for Our Lands

Imagine a vibrant symphony of flames, carefully orchestrated to breathe life back into our landscapes. This is the essence of prescribed burning, a practice where fire, once feared, becomes a tool of renewal. It's a dance with nature, guided by science and a deep respect for the land.

Whispers from the Past, Lessons for Today

For millennia, Indigenous communities have understood the power of fire. They wielded it as a brushstroke, shaping ecosystems and fostering biodiversity. Today, we're rediscovering this ancient wisdom, embracing controlled burns as a vital land management tool.

The Science of the Flame

Prescribed burning isn't about unleashing chaos; it's about harnessing the transformative power of fire. Think of it as a reset button for nature. By carefully applying fire under specific conditions, we can:

Cleanse and Rejuvenate: Just as a sculptor chisels away excess stone, prescribed burns remove the buildup of flammable debris, reducing the risk of catastrophic wildfires.
Nourish the Soil: Fire unlocks nutrients trapped in dead plants, returning them to the earth like a gift. This revitalizes the soil, promoting new growth and a vibrant tapestry of life.
Shape the Landscape: Different plants and animals have unique relationships with fire. Some thrive in its wake, while others depend on it for survival. Prescribed burns help create a mosaic of habitats, supporting a rich diversity of species.
A Choreography of Care

Prescribed burning is a delicate dance, requiring careful planning and execution. Experts meticulously assess the land, weather, and potential impacts before striking the first match. They use a variety of techniques, from gentle backfires to more intense headfires, carefully guiding the flames to achieve specific goals.

Beyond the Burn

The benefits of prescribed burning extend far beyond the immediate flames. By reducing wildfire risk, we safeguard homes, communities, and precious natural resources. We create healthier forests, more resilient ecosystems, and a legacy of stewardship for future generations.

Challenges and Opportunities

Prescribed burning isn't without its challenges. Smoke management, public perception, and the complexities of changing climate conditions require ongoing attention and innovation. But with careful planning and collaboration, we can overcome these hurdles and embrace the full potential of this powerful tool.

A Call to Action

Prescribed burning is a testament to our ability to work in harmony with nature. It's a reminder that fire, when wielded with respect and understanding, can be a force for good. Let's continue to explore, refine, and champion this practice, ensuring a vibrant future for our lands and the life they sustain.

　　　Subtopic 4: Where Smoke Once Meant Harmony: Learning from Ancient Fire Wisdom

Imagine a world where fire isn't a fearsome enemy, but a trusted friend. For Indigenous peoples across the globe, this wasn't a fairytale, but a reality crafted over millennia. They wielded fire not with fear, but with an intimate understanding of its dance – a practice we call cultural burning.

Think of it as a conversation with the land, a way to whisper to the grasses and trees. Western fire management often shouts "No!" to fire, trying to extinguish it. But cultural burning listens, responding with carefully placed flames that nurture, rather than destroy.

Whispers of the Past: How Ancient Fires Shaped the Land

Cultural burning isn't just about striking a match. It's a symphony of knowledge passed down through generations, a deep connection to the land's rhythm. Each Indigenous community has its own unique melody, but some harmonious notes resonate across cultures:

Gentle Flames: Instead of raging infernos, cultural burns are like warm breaths over the land. They prune, rather than incinerate, encouraging new life to sprout.
A Patchwork Quilt: Imagine a landscape woven with fire, a mosaic of burned and unburned patches. This creates a vibrant tapestry of habitats, a haven for diverse life.
Nature's Clock: Cultural burning follows the pulse of the seasons, knowing when flames will coax forth seeds or guide animals on their journeys.
A Purpose in Every Spark: Each fire has a goal – whether it's coaxing berries to ripen, creating clearings for game, or ensuring the forest stays healthy.
Stories from the Embers: Cultural Burning Around the World

Australia's Ancient Songlines: For over 65,000 years, Aboriginal Australians have woven fire into their very being. They paint the landscape with flames, coaxing kangaroos to grazing grounds and ensuring the land bursts with bush tucker (food).

North America's Whispering Pines: Native American tribes, like the Karuk in California, tend their forests with fire, ensuring hazelnuts flourish and materials for intricate baskets abound. In the Southeast, the Muscogee (Creek) Nation kept pine savannas open, perfect for hunting and growing crops.
Amazonia's Living Tapestry: Deep in the Amazon, Indigenous peoples use fire like an artist's brush, creating a mosaic of forest and open spaces, ensuring the rainforest thrives in all its diversity.
The Gifts of Fire: Why Cultural Burning Matters

When we listen to the wisdom of cultural burning, we discover a treasure trove of benefits:

Taming the Wildfire: By keeping fuels in check and creating fire-resistant landscapes, cultural burning helps prevent those devastating megafires that make headlines.
Nature's Abundance: A symphony of flames creates a richer, more diverse ecosystem. More plants, more animals, more life flourishing in all its glory.
A Healthy Pulse: Fire, when wielded with care, can actually make the land healthier. It nourishes the soil, helps nutrients flow, and even keeps invasive species at bay.
Keeping Culture Alive: For many Indigenous communities, fire is woven into their ceremonies, stories, and identity. Reviving these practices helps keep those ancient traditions burning bright.
Bridging the Gap: Bringing Ancient Wisdom to Modern Fire Management

While the benefits of cultural burning are clear, rekindling this ancient practice isn't without its challenges:

Scars of Suppression: Decades of aggressively putting out every fire have disrupted traditional practices and led to the loss of precious knowledge.

Building Trust: We need to heal the wounds of the past and build genuine partnerships between Indigenous communities and government agencies.
Outdated Rules: Our laws need to catch up and recognize the wisdom of Indigenous fire stewardship.
A Changing Climate: With wildfires becoming fiercer and more frequent, we need all the tools in our toolbox, including the ancient wisdom of cultural burning.
Seeds of Hope: Opportunities for a Brighter Future

Sharing the Knowledge: Let's create spaces where Indigenous communities, scientists, and land managers can come together, learn from each other, and find common ground.
Changing the Rules: We need policies that respect and support Indigenous fire practices, allowing cultural burning to flourish once again.
Empowering Communities: Investing in training and education programs can help Indigenous communities reclaim their fire wisdom and lead the way.
Adapting to Change: By blending ancient knowledge with modern science, we can create fire management strategies that are resilient in the face of climate change.
Shining Examples: Where Cultural Burning is Making a Comeback

The Karuk Tribe's Revival: In California, the Karuk Tribe is working hand-in-hand with agencies to bring back cultural burning, showing how collaboration can heal the land and strengthen communities.
Australia's Firesticks Alliance: This Indigenous-led organization is rekindling the flames of cultural burning across Australia, empowering communities to care for their country with fire.
Montana's Tribal Wisdom: The Confederated Salish and Kootenai Tribes are weaving traditional knowledge with

Aging in Place, Perishing in Place: Grandma Emily, her walker gathering dust, watches the flames approach, her lifeline – the senior center van – cut off by road closures. For the elderly and disabled, wildfire becomes a cruel test of mobility, a race against time they're destined to lose.

2. Beyond the Burning Embers:

Whispers in the Wind: The crackle of the scanner, the frantic texts, the emergency alerts that never arrive. For those without internet access, reliable transportation, or language support, vital information becomes a phantom, leaving them stranded in the inferno.

Scars on the Soul: The trauma runs deep, etched in the faces of children coughing on smoke, in the eyes of firefighters battling exhaustion and despair. Wildfire leaves wounds that don't heal easily, a mental health crisis simmering beneath the ashes.

3. Seeds of Resilience:

The Fire Within: In the charred ruins of Paradise, California, a community rises from the ashes. Neighbors helping neighbors, rebuilding stronger, fire-wise homes, creating defensible spaces, and demanding better from their leaders.

Ancient Wisdom, Modern Solutions: Indigenous communities, stewards of the land for millennia, hold the key to living with fire. Their controlled burns, their knowledge of the ecosystem, offer a path forward, a way to heal the land and protect those most vulnerable.

This is not a story of despair, but a call to action. We can map the vulnerabilities, yes, but we must also map the solutions. Empower communities, bridge the gaps in resources, and weave resilience into the very fabric of our society. Let the flames of wildfire ignite a fire within us – a fire of compassion, innovation, and unwavering commitment to protect those who need it most.

What can you do?

Educate yourself: Learn about wildfire risks in your area and how to prepare.
Support vulnerable communities: Volunteer, donate, or advocate for policies that address the root causes of vulnerability.
Demand change: Hold elected officials accountable for investing in fire prevention, community resilience, and equitable disaster response.

The time to act is now, before the next ember ignites a catastrophe.

The Political Economy of Wildfire Risk

Imagine a world where the very ground beneath your feet could ignite, turning your home, your community, your life into ash. This is the reality for millions living in wildfire-prone areas. But the threat isn't distributed equally. Historical injustices and systemic inequalities have created a wildfire burden disproportionately borne by marginalized communities.

Redlining: A Legacy of Vulnerability

In the past, discriminatory practices like redlining literally drew lines on maps, denying essential services to predominantly Black and minority neighborhoods. This created a domino effect: disinvestment, limited economic opportunities, and reduced access to resources. Today, these communities often find themselves in the path of wildfires, lacking the means to adequately prepare or recover.

Trapped by Inequality

Discriminatory housing policies have historically pushed marginalized communities into less desirable areas, often with higher wildfire risk. These areas may be close to wildland-urban interfaces, have limited infrastructure, or lack adequate fire protection services. It's like being trapped in a game where the rules are rigged against you.

Unequal Resources, Unequal Outcomes

Imagine trying to fight a fire with a bucket of water while your neighbor has a fire hose. This illustrates the disparity in resources between marginalized communities and more affluent ones. Limited access to healthcare, education, and financial capital can hinder the ability to prepare for, respond to, and recover from wildfires.

The Oakland Hills Firestorm (1991): A Stark Reminder

The Oakland Hills Firestorm tragically demonstrated the unequal impacts of wildfires. Low-income and minority communities were disproportionately affected, living in older, more flammable homes with limited access to evacuation routes. The fire exposed the deep scars of inequality.

The Camp Fire (2018): Paradise Lost

The Camp Fire, California's deadliest and most destructive wildfire, ravaged the town of Paradise. A significant portion of the population was elderly and low-income, many unable to evacuate in time due to limited mobility, lack of transportation, and inadequate warning systems. The fire revealed the vulnerability of those left behind.

The 2020 Western Wildfire Season: A Wake-Up Call

The 2020 Western Wildfire Season was a stark reminder of the unequal impacts of wildfires. Farmworkers, undocumented immigrants, and indigenous communities faced immense challenges in accessing information, evacuation resources, and healthcare services. Their voices often go unheard, their struggles unseen.

Policy for a Just Future

We need a multi-pronged approach to address the political economy of wildfire risk. Investing in equitable mitigation and adaptation strategies, addressing historical injustices, promoting equitable access to resources, and empowering marginalized communities are crucial steps.

Wildfires don't discriminate, but our systems do. By acknowledging the role of power and inequality, we can work towards a future where all communities are resilient to the impacts of wildfires.

When the Flames Come Calling: Stories of Resilience from the Firelines

"This," says Maria, her voice trembling slightly, "is all I have left." The photo shows a laughing family in front of a modest cabin, now reduced to ashes. Maria's story isn't unique. Across the American West, wildfires are raging with increasing ferocity, leaving a trail of devastation and displacement in their wake. But these fires don't burn equally. They expose the raw edges of inequality, tearing through communities already grappling with poverty, discrimination, and neglect.

This isn't just a story about flames and smoke. It's about the people caught in the inferno – families forced to flee their homes, elders struggling to evacuate, firefighters battling exhaustion and despair. It's about the deep-rooted injustices that make some communities far more vulnerable than others.

But amidst the ashes, embers of hope are glowing. Communities are rising from the ruins, armed with knowledge, innovation, and an unyielding spirit of resilience.

For the Karuk Tribe, fire isn't just a force of destruction, it's a sacred tool. For centuries, they've used controlled burns to shape the land, nurture biodiversity, and protect their communities. Now, their ancestral knowledge is guiding a new era of fire management, one that blends tradition with science.

(Shift to an interactive map: Users can zoom in on different regions to explore community-led wildfire resilience initiatives. Clicking on an icon reveals photos, videos, and descriptions of projects like neighborhood wildfire preparedness groups, community resilience hubs, and local food systems.)

Across the country, communities are taking action. Neighbors are banding together to create defensible spaces, volunteers are staffing fire departments, and Indigenous tribes are reclaiming their role as stewards of the land.

"We lost everything," she says, her voice filled with emotion, "but we didn't lose each other." Her story is a testament to the power of community, the strength of the human spirit, and the unwavering belief in a brighter future.

The flames may come calling, but we will not be consumed. Together, we can build a future where wildfires are no longer a threat to our communities, but a force of renewal and resilience.

Environmental Justice in Wildfire Management: Advocating for Fair and Equitable Protection for All Communities

Wildfires, a natural part of many ecosystems, have become increasingly frequent and destructive due to climate change and human activities. While wildfires play a role in forest health, their impacts are not felt equally across all communities. Low-income communities, communities of color, Indigenous communities, and rural communities often bear the brunt of wildfire devastation, highlighting the urgent need for environmental justice in wildfire management.

Environmental justice is the principle that all people, regardless of race, color, national origin, or income, have the right to equal protection from environmental hazards and the right to participate in decisions that affect their environment. In the context of wildfire management, this means ensuring that all communities have equal access to resources, information, and decision-making power, and that wildfire mitigation and recovery efforts are conducted in a way that is equitable and just.

Key Principles and Practices of Environmental Justice in Wildfire Management:

Recognition of Disproportionate Impacts: Acknowledging that the risks and impacts of wildfires are not evenly distributed, with marginalized and vulnerable communities facing greater vulnerability.

Meaningful Community Participation: Involving all affected communities in planning processes, sharing their knowledge and concerns, and contributing to decision-making.

Equitable Distribution of Resources: Allocating resources for wildfire mitigation, preparedness, response, and recovery equitably, prioritizing communities most at risk.

Access to Information and Education: Providing clear, accurate, and timely information about wildfire risks, preparedness measures, evacuation procedures, and recovery resources in accessible formats for all communities.

Cultural Sensitivity: Respecting the cultural values, traditions, and knowledge systems of Indigenous and other communities in wildfire management practices.

Importance of Community Participation and Empowerment:

Community participation is crucial for effective wildfire management. Local communities possess valuable knowledge about their environment, vulnerabilities, and capacities. Their insights can inform the development of more effective and culturally appropriate wildfire management strategies. Empowering communities to participate in decision-making fosters a sense of ownership and responsibility, leading to greater community buy-in and support for wildfire management initiatives. It also helps build trust between communities and agencies, essential for collaboration in wildfire preparedness and response.

Strategies for Promoting Environmental Justice in Wildfire Management:

Community-Based Wildfire Risk Assessments: Conducting participatory risk assessments to identify hazards, vulnerabilities, and capacities, tailored to the specific needs and concerns of different communities.

Collaborative Wildfire Management Planning: Establishing collaborative planning processes that bring together diverse stakeholders, including community members, government agencies, scientists, and land managers.

Capacity Building and Resource Sharing: Investing in capacity building programs to empower communities with the knowledge, skills, and resources to participate effectively in wildfire management.

Equitable Funding and Resource Allocation: Developing funding mechanisms that prioritize the needs of vulnerable communities and ensure equitable distribution of resources.

Culturally Appropriate Wildfire Management Practices: Incorporating traditional ecological knowledge and cultural practices into wildfire management strategies.

Examples and Case Studies:

The Karuk Tribe and Prescribed Burning in California: The Karuk Tribe's efforts to revitalize their traditional burning practices demonstrate the effectiveness of traditional ecological knowledge and the importance of recognizing Indigenous sovereignty and self-determination in wildfire management.

Community Wildfire Protection Plans in Colorado: These plans, developed through a collaborative process, help ensure that wildfire mitigation efforts are tailored to the specific needs and priorities of each community.

Addressing Environmental Injustice in Wildfire Recovery in Oregon: The state of Oregon has implemented initiatives to address environmental injustice in wildfire recovery, including providing targeted assistance to vulnerable communities and ensuring equitable recovery efforts.

Challenges and Opportunities:

Challenges include historical inequities, power imbalances, limited resources, and the impacts of climate change. However, there are also opportunities, such as growing awareness of environmental justice, community-led initiatives, technological advances, and potential policy changes.

Conclusion:

Environmental justice is essential for ensuring that all communities are treated fairly and have the opportunity to participate in wildfire management decisions that affect their lives and livelihoods. By embracing the principles of environmental justice, we can create a more equitable and resilient wildfire management system that protects all communities. This requires ongoing commitment and collaboration among diverse stakeholders. By working together, we can build a future where wildfire management is just, equitable, and sustainable for all.

Citizen Scientists on the Fire Lines: Harnessing Community Power for Wildfire Resilience

Eyes on the Ground: How Everyday Heroes are Joining the Fight Against Wildfires

Wildfires are a global threat that's growing fiercer every year, fueled by climate change and human actions. While traditional monitoring systems are vital, they can be limited in their reach and responsiveness. This is where citizen science steps in, offering a powerful and budget-friendly way to enhance wildfire monitoring and early detection. By harnessing the collective power of dedicated volunteers, we can create a more vigilant and responsive network to combat this growing menace.

Citizen Science: Everyday People Making a Difference

Citizen science involves public participation in scientific research, allowing individuals to contribute to data collection, analysis, and problem-solving. In the context of wildfire monitoring, this means empowering communities to become active participants in protecting their surroundings.

Technology: The Citizen Scientist's Toolkit

Technology plays a crucial role in facilitating citizen science initiatives for wildfire monitoring. Here are some key aspects:

   Mobile Apps and Platforms: Dedicated mobile applications and online platforms serve as central hubs for citizen scientists. These platforms enable users to:

Report fire sightings in real-time, including location, size, and visual evidence (photos/videos).

Submit observations on weather conditions, fuel loads, and potential fire hazards.

Access educational resources and safety guidelines.

Connect with other volunteers and researchers.

Remote Sensing and Drones: Advancements in remote sensing technologies, including satellite imagery and drones, provide valuable data for wildfire monitoring. Citizen scientists can contribute by:

Ground-truthing satellite data: Validating satellite-detected fire hotspots by providing on-the-ground observations.

Piloting drones equipped with thermal cameras to identify fire starts in remote areas.

Analyzing aerial imagery to assess fire spread and damage.

Sensors and IoT Devices: The Internet of Things (IoT) offers opportunities for deploying networks of sensors to monitor environmental conditions relevant to wildfire risk. Citizen scientists can be involved in:

Deploying and maintaining low-cost sensors that measure temperature, humidity, and wind speed.

Collecting data from sensor networks and contributing to real-time fire risk maps.

Developing and testing new sensor technologies for improved accuracy and coverage.

Artificial Intelligence (AI) and Machine Learning (ML): AI and ML algorithms can be used to analyze large datasets collected by citizen scientists, identify patterns, and predict fire risk. This can help in:

Automating the verification of citizen-submitted fire reports.

Identifying high-risk areas based on historical data and real-time conditions.

Optimizing resource allocation for fire suppression efforts.

Benefits of Citizen Science for Wildfire Monitoring

Increased Coverage: Citizen scientists can expand the reach of monitoring efforts, particularly in remote or underserved areas where traditional resources may be limited.

Early Detection: By being present in the landscape, citizen scientists can often detect fires in their early stages, enabling rapid response and potentially preventing larger conflagrations.

Cost-Effectiveness: Citizen science provides a cost-effective way to gather valuable data and supplement traditional monitoring systems.

Community Engagement: Engaging communities in wildfire monitoring fosters a sense of ownership and responsibility, leading to increased awareness and preparedness.

Data Quality: While concerns about data quality exist, studies have shown that with proper training and validation, citizen science data can be highly reliable and valuable for scientific research.

Challenges and Considerations

Data Accuracy and Validation: Ensuring the accuracy and reliability of data collected by citizen scientists is crucial. This requires:

Providing comprehensive training and clear protocols for data collection.

Implementing data validation mechanisms, such as expert review or cross-validation with other sources.

Utilizing technology to automate data quality checks and identify potential errors.

Volunteer Recruitment and Retention: Maintaining a consistent and engaged volunteer base can be challenging. Strategies for recruitment and retention include:

Offering incentives, such as recognition, training opportunities, and access to exclusive data.

Building a strong community through online forums, events, and social media engagement.

Providing clear roles and responsibilities for volunteers, ensuring their contributions are valued.

Technology Access and Literacy: Not all communities have equal access to technology and digital literacy skills. Addressing this requires:

Providing training and support for using technology platforms and tools.

Exploring alternative methods for data collection and reporting, such as paper-based forms or SMS messaging.

Partnering with community organizations to reach underserved populations.

Safety and Liability: Ensuring the safety of citizen scientists involved in wildfire monitoring is paramount. This involves:

Providing comprehensive safety training and guidelines.

Establishing clear communication protocols and emergency procedures.

Addressing liability concerns through waivers and insurance policies.

Case Studies and Examples

Australia: The Country Fire Authority (CFA) in Victoria, Australia, has a long history of engaging volunteers in wildfire response. In recent years, they have incorporated citizen science approaches, utilizing mobile apps for fire reporting and community-based monitoring programs.

California, USA: The UC Berkeley Center for Fire Research and Outreach has developed several citizen science initiatives, including the "Fire Chasers" program, which trains volunteers to collect data on fire behavior and fuel conditions.

Spain: The Pau Costa Foundation has implemented a citizen science program using drones to monitor fire risk in Mediterranean forests. Volunteers are trained to pilot drones and collect aerial imagery for analysis.

Indonesia: The Rainforest Connection utilizes old cell phones repurposed as acoustic sensors to detect illegal logging and fire activity in rainforests. Citizen scientists help monitor the audio data and report potential threats.

The Future of Citizen Science in Wildfire Monitoring

The future of citizen science in wildfire monitoring is promising, with continued advancements in technology and growing public awareness. We can expect to see:

Increased integration of AI and ML: AI and ML will play a greater role in automating data analysis, identifying patterns, and predicting fire risk.

More sophisticated sensor networks: The development of new sensor technologies and the expansion of IoT networks will enable more comprehensive and real-time monitoring of environmental conditions.

Enhanced community engagement: Citizen science programs will become more integrated into community-based disaster preparedness and response efforts.

Global collaboration: International collaborations and data sharing will facilitate the development of more effective wildfire monitoring strategies on a global scale.

Citizen science has the potential to revolutionize wildfire monitoring and early detection, empowering communities to become active participants in protecting their environment. By embracing technology, fostering collaboration, and addressing the challenges, we can harness the collective power of citizen scientists to combat the growing threat of wildfires.

Citizen Science: Igniting a Revolution in Wildfire Defense

Forget the lone scientist in a lab coat. Today, the front lines of wildfire defense are being redefined by everyday heroes – hikers, bird watchers, photographers, even gamers – armed with smartphones, a passion for their communities, and the power of citizen science.

Imagine a world where a hiker on a trail, snapping a photo of dry brush with their phone, becomes an invaluable data point in a complex fire prediction model. Picture a birdwatcher, reporting a wisp of smoke through an app, triggering a rapid response that stops a wildfire in its tracks. This is the power of citizen science, a movement that's turning ordinary people into a force for wildfire resilience.

1. Fueling the Fire Models: Citizen Scientists on the Ground (and in the Cloud)

Fire behavior models, the crystal balls of wildfire prediction, are hungry for data. They crave information on everything from the type of trees in a forest to the moisture content of the underbrush. And that's where citizen scientists come in, acting as the eyes and ears on the ground (and even in the sky!).

Trailblazers with Smartphones: Imagine a network of volunteers, trained by local fire officials, hiking through a national park. They're using a special app to identify different types of trees and underbrush, marking areas with heavy fuel loads that could become fire hazards. This information feeds directly into fire behavior models, giving firefighters a crucial edge in predicting a fire's path.

Sky-High Detectives: Drones equipped with high-resolution cameras, piloted by trained citizen scientists, soar over vast landscapes, capturing images that reveal hidden fire risks. These aerial scouts provide a bird's-eye view of vulnerable areas, helping firefighters prioritize fuel management efforts.

Virtual Fire Watch: Gamers, putting their skills to a new purpose, analyze satellite imagery and aerial photos in a virtual reality environment, identifying areas with dry vegetation or potential ignition sources. Their virtual patrols contribute to a real-world understanding of fire risk.

2. Risk Assessment: Mapping Vulnerability, Empowering Communities

Knowing where a fire might start is only half the battle. Understanding which communities are most vulnerable is crucial for effective wildfire preparedness. Citizen scientists are stepping up to map the human side of fire risk.

Community Vulnerability Detectives: Volunteers, armed with surveys and a knack for observation, walk through neighborhoods, noting factors like building materials, evacuation routes, and the presence of elderly or disabled residents. This information helps create detailed vulnerability maps, guiding evacuation plans and resource allocation.

The Wildland-Urban Interface (WUI) Explorers: The WUI, where homes meet wildlands, is a tinderbox waiting to ignite. Citizen scientists, using GPS devices and online mapping tools, meticulously trace the boundaries of the WUI, identifying areas where homes are most exposed to wildfire.

History Keepers: Local residents, passionate about their community's past, delve into archives and oral histories, piecing together a timeline of past fires. This historical perspective helps understand long-term fire patterns and predict future risks.

3. Resource Allocation: Putting Out Fires with People Power

When a wildfire erupts, every second counts. Citizen scientists are becoming a vital part of the rapid response network, helping firefighters get to the right place at the right time.

The Real-Time Fire Spotters: Imagine a network of fire lookouts, not just staffed by professionals, but also by volunteers with a keen eye and a dedicated app. These citizen spotters provide immediate alerts, giving firefighters a head start on containing a blaze.

Fuel Management Task Force: Armed with data collected by fellow citizen scientists, community groups organize fuel reduction projects, clearing brush and creating fire breaks around vulnerable areas. They become a proactive force in wildfire defense.

Post-Fire Recovery Partners: After the flames subside, citizen scientists don't rest. They monitor erosion, track vegetation recovery, and help assess the effectiveness of restoration efforts, ensuring that their community rises stronger from the ashes.

Challenges and Opportunities: Building a Future Where Communities and Science Unite

The citizen science movement faces hurdles, from ensuring data accuracy to managing vast amounts of information. But the opportunities are immense.

AI and the Citizen Science Supercharge: Imagine artificial intelligence algorithms sifting through millions of data points contributed by citizen scientists, identifying patterns and predicting fire behavior with unprecedented accuracy.

Virtual Reality Fire Drills: Communities gather in virtual reality landscapes, experiencing simulated wildfire scenarios and practicing evacuation strategies. This immersive technology transforms wildfire preparedness from a lecture into an engaging experience.

By embracing innovation, fostering collaboration, and empowering individuals, we can unlock the full potential of citizen science. It's a future where communities and science unite to build a safer, more fire-resilient world.

Empowering Communities to Fight Fire: The Role of Community-Based Fire Brigades

In many parts of the world, community-based fire brigades (CBBs) play a vital role in protecting homes and neighborhoods, especially in areas with limited access to professional fire services. These brigades are made up of local residents who are trained to prevent, prepare for, and respond to fire incidents. They empower communities to take ownership of their fire safety and build local resilience.

The Importance of Community-Based Fire Brigades

CBBs are crucial in areas where professional fire services are limited or nonexistent. This can be due to various factors, including:

   Remote locations: Many rural communities are far from professional fire stations, making quick response difficult.
   Limited resources: Some communities may lack the funds to support a full-time fire department.
   Difficult terrain: In certain areas, terrain can hinder access for fire trucks.

In these situations, CBBs provide a vital first line of defense. They can help prevent fires from starting and respond quickly to extinguish fires before they spread.

Key Roles and Responsibilities of CBBs

CBBs typically have a range of responsibilities, including:

   Fire prevention: Educating the community about fire safety and prevention through home safety inspections, fire safety classes for children, and community events.

Fire preparedness: Developing evacuation plans, organizing fire drills, and maintaining fire-fighting equipment.

Fire suppression: Responding to fire incidents and using basic fire-fighting equipment to extinguish fires and protect lives and property.

Community engagement: Building community resilience by fostering a sense of ownership and responsibility for fire safety.

Examples of Successful Community-Based Fire Brigades

There are many successful CBB programs worldwide, such as:

The Paulo Freire Community Fire Brigade in Brazil: Formed in 2003 in Porto Alegre, this brigade has reduced fire incidents through fire prevention education, community engagement, and fire suppression.

The Community Fire Brigades of South Africa: Established in 2007 to address informal settlement fires, this program has trained over 1,000 community members in fire prevention and suppression techniques.

The Fire Safe Councils of California: A network of over 1,000 community-based organizations that work to reduce wildfire risk in California, providing fire prevention education, community wildfire protection planning, and wildfire preparedness training.

Building Local Capacity and Resilience

CBBs play a crucial role in building local capacity and resilience to fire. By empowering communities to take ownership of their fire safety, they create safer and more resilient communities.

CBBs build local capacity and resilience by:

   Providing knowledge and skills: Training community members in fire safety, prevention, and suppression techniques.
   Fostering community ownership: Creating a sense of shared responsibility for fire prevention and response.
   Strengthening social cohesion: Building trust and cooperation among community members through collaborative efforts.
   Developing local leadership: Empowering community members to take on leadership roles in fire safety management.

Challenges and Opportunities for Community-Based Fire Brigades

While CBBs offer significant benefits, they also face challenges, such as:

   Funding: Securing adequate funding for equipment, training, and operations can be difficult.
   Training: Providing comprehensive training to CBB members can be challenging.
   Equipment: Access to adequate equipment is essential for effective fire response.
   Coordination: Coordinating with professional fire services can be challenging.

Despite these challenges, there are opportunities for CBBs to grow and strengthen their impact:

   Technology: Utilizing new technologies like mobile apps, drones, and social media to improve effectiveness and awareness.

Partnerships: Partnering with professional fire services, NGOs, and government agencies to access resources, training, and support.

Community engagement: Engaging with communities through social media, events, and school programs to raise awareness and foster participation.

Conclusion

Community-based fire brigades are a vital part of fire management. They empower communities to take ownership of their fire safety, creating safer and more resilient communities. By investing in CBBs, we can build a stronger and more prepared fire defense for all.

Additional Resources

International Association of Fire Chiefs (IAFC): https://www.iafc.org/
National Fire Protection Association (NFPA): https://www.nfpa.org/en
Ready.gov: https://www.ready.gov/
The Paulo Freire Community Fire Brigade: https://freire.org/ (website in Portuguese)
The Community Fire Brigades of South Africa: https://www.cgfa.co.za/
The Fire Safe Councils of California: https://cafiresafecouncil.org/

Bridging the Gap: Where Wildfire Wisdom Meets Citizen Passion

Okay, let's be real – wildfires are a raging beast. They're fierce, unpredictable, and they don't care about boundaries. We need all hands on deck to tackle this fiery foe, and that means bringing together the pros with the passionate folks on the ground – our citizen scientists.

The Hidden Poison: Contamination Lurks in the Ashes

But the damage goes deeper than just sediment. Wildfires unleash a cocktail of contaminants into our water systems, a hidden threat that can have devastating consequences for human health and the environment.

Think of heavy metals like lead and mercury, leaching from the ashes and seeping into our drinking water. Imagine cancer-causing chemicals, released from burning homes and infrastructure, finding their way into our rivers and streams. And then there are the fire retardants, meant to protect us, but potentially harming aquatic life and contaminating our water supplies.

A Vicious Cycle: Wildfires and Water Scarcity

The consequences of wildfire-induced water contamination are far-reaching. Treatment plants struggle to remove these pollutants, and the cost of providing safe drinking water skyrockets. In some cases, entire communities are left without access to clean water, forced to rely on emergency supplies.

And as wildfires become more frequent and intense, the strain on our water resources will only worsen. Reservoirs will shrink, and irrigation systems will falter, threatening agriculture and food security. The very lifeblood of our communities, our water, is under attack.

Turning the Tide: A Call for Action

But there is hope. By understanding the complex relationship between wildfires and water, we can take steps to protect this precious resource. We can implement better forest management practices, invest in erosion

Subtopic 4: Water for Fire, Fire for Water: A Symbiotic Dance to Tame the Flames and Quench the Thirst

In the arid landscapes of the American West, where the sun beats down with relentless intensity, two formidable forces are locked in a delicate and dangerous dance: wildfire and water scarcity. These intertwined threats, like two sides of the same coin, demand our attention and a unified approach to their management.

Wildfires, with their insatiable hunger, consume vast stretches of land, leaving behind a trail of destruction. But their impact extends far beyond the charred remains of trees and homes. They poison our precious water sources, choking rivers and lakes with sediment and ash, rendering them unfit for life. The very water we need to fight these infernos becomes a casualty of their wrath.

Water, the lifeblood of our planet, is also a powerful ally in the battle against wildfire. Healthy forests, nourished by abundant water, act as natural firebreaks, slowing the spread of flames. Yet, in the face of drought, these same forests become tinderboxes, ready to ignite with the slightest spark.

The intricate connection between wildfire and water is undeniable. We can no longer afford to treat them as separate entities, managed in isolation. Instead, we must embrace a holistic approach, one that recognizes their interdependence and seeks to harmonize their relationship.

A New Paradigm: Integrating Water and Wildfire Management

Imagine a world where water and fire coexist in balance, where forests thrive, and communities are protected from the ravages of both drought and wildfire. This vision is within our reach, but it requires a paradigm shift in our thinking and our actions.

We must move beyond the traditional silos of water management and fire suppression and embrace a new era of integrated management. This means:

Restoring Forests and Watersheds: Thinning overgrown forests, conducting prescribed burns, and restoring riparian areas can reduce fuel loads, improve water infiltration, and enhance the resilience of our landscapes.

Conserving Water: Implementing water-efficient irrigation practices, harvesting rainwater, and recharging groundwater aquifers can help maintain healthy vegetation, which acts as a natural firebreak.

Managing Fire Wisely: Developing community wildfire protection plans, creating Firewise landscapes around homes, and adopting an integrated fire management approach that balances suppression with the ecological role of fire can help minimize the risk of large, destructive wildfires.

Harnessing Technology: Utilizing remote sensing, advanced modeling tools, and early warning systems can help us better understand and manage the complex interactions between wildfire and water.

Fostering Collaboration: Building strong partnerships among agencies, organizations, and communities is essential for effective integrated management.

Case Studies: Where Water and Fire Dance in Harmony

The Sierra Nevada Watershed Improvement Program (SNWIP): In the majestic Sierra Nevada mountains, a collaborative effort is underway to restore forest health and improve water quality. By thinning forests, conducting prescribed burns, and restoring meadows, SNWIP is reducing wildfire risk, enhancing water infiltration, and increasing streamflows.

The Four Forest Restoration Initiative (4FRI): Across 2.4 million acres of ponderosa pine forests in Arizona, 4FRI is working to create a more resilient landscape through thinning and prescribed burns. The project also incorporates watershed protection measures, such as erosion control and riparian restoration, to ensure that restoration activities benefit water resources.

The Deschutes River Conservancy: In the Deschutes River Basin of Oregon, the Deschutes River Conservancy is restoring riparian areas and improving water quality. By working with landowners, agencies, and other stakeholders, the Conservancy is creating natural firebreaks and protecting water resources, while also enhancing wildlife habitat.

Challenges and Opportunities

The path towards integrated water and wildfire management is not without its challenges. Limited resources, conflicting priorities, and the ever-present threat of climate change all pose significant obstacles.

However, there are also tremendous opportunities. Increased collaboration, technological advancements, and growing public awareness can all help us overcome these challenges and create a more sustainable future.

Conclusion: A Call to Action

The future of our water resources and the health of our forests are inextricably linked. By embracing an integrated approach to water and wildfire management, we can build more resilient landscapes that benefit both people and the environment.

The Lingering Haze: Unveiling the Long-Term Health Effects of Wildfire Smoke

The air crackles with a strange, acrid taste. It's not the familiar scent of autumn leaves burning, but something more sinister – the ghost of wildfires past, clinging to your lungs with each inhaled breath. These aren't just fleeting coughs and scratchy throats; we're talking about insidious, long-term damage that lurks in the shadows long after the flames have died down.

Imagine your lungs as a once-pristine forest, now choked with smoke and ash. The delicate branches of your airways, once supple and free, become stiff and brittle, struggling to draw in the life-giving oxygen. This is the reality of chronic respiratory diseases like COPD, where every breath becomes a battle. Wildfire smoke isn't just a trigger for those already suffering; it's a cruel accomplice, hastening the decline and turning a slow burn into a raging inferno.

Think of asthma as a wildfire within your own body. The airways, inflamed and hypersensitive, constrict like panicked crowds fleeing a burning building. Wildfire smoke fans these flames, turning a manageable condition into a life-threatening crisis. And for those who've never experienced the terror of an asthma attack, smoke can be the spark that ignites a lifelong struggle.

Then there's the silent killer – lung cancer. We all know the dangers of smoking, but wildfire smoke carries its own carcinogenic cocktail. Invisible toxins, like microscopic assassins, infiltrate the deepest recesses of your lungs, leaving behind a trail of cellular damage that can fester for years before manifesting as a deadly tumor.

This isn't just about statistics and case studies; it's about real people, real lives. The firefighter battling blazes, only to find herself battling for each breath years later. The child growing up in a smoke-filled world, their young lungs scarred before they've even had a chance to fully develop.

We can't just stand by and watch as wildfire smoke steals our breath and our future. We need to fight fire with knowledge, arming ourselves with information about the risks and taking action to protect ourselves and our loved ones. This means demanding better air quality monitoring, investing in research, and supporting policies that address climate change, the root cause of this growing threat.

The air we breathe is a shared resource, a precious gift. It's time we started treating it that way, before the consequences become irreversible.

The Heart of the Inferno: When Wildfire Smoke Turns Deadly

Imagine a dragon, not of myth, but of stark reality, its fiery breath sweeping across the land, leaving behind a trail of destruction. This isn't a scene from a fantasy novel, but the grim reality of wildfires, a growing menace in our warming world. While the immediate devastation is all too visible, a more insidious threat lingers in the air – wildfire smoke. This invisible enemy doesn't just choke our lungs; it strikes at the very core of our being, our hearts.

Unmasking the Invisible Enemy: The Toxic Cocktail in Wildfire Smoke

Picture this: a microscopic army of invaders, PM2.5 particles, so tiny they can slip past our body's defenses, infiltrating deep into our lungs and bloodstream. These aren't lone wolves; they're part of a motley crew of noxious gases like carbon monoxide and volatile organic compounds, each with its own sinister agenda. Together, they form a toxic cocktail that wreaks havoc on our cardiovascular system.

The Smoke Signals: How Wildfire Smoke Attacks Our Hearts

Think of our cardiovascular system as a complex highway network, with blood vessels as the roads and the heart as the central hub. Wildfire smoke throws this intricate system into disarray, like a sudden traffic jam on a busy freeway.

    Inflammation Nation: The PM2.5 invaders trigger a red alert in our bodies, unleashing an inflammatory storm. This isn't just a localized battle in the lungs; the inflammation spreads like wildfire, reaching the heart and blood vessels, setting the stage for plaque buildup and clogged arteries.

    Oxidative Stress: The Cellular Siege: Wildfire smoke is packed with oxidants, cellular saboteurs that damage our delicate tissues. This oxidative stress weakens our blood vessels, making them prone to leaks and blockages, like a crumbling road riddled with potholes.

    The Nervous System Breakdown: The autonomic nervous system, our body's autopilot for heart rate and blood pressure, goes haywire under the smoke's influence. It's like a faulty traffic light system, causing erratic heart rhythms and blood pressure spikes, increasing the risk of accidents.

    Endothelial Dysfunction: The Roadblock: The endothelium, the inner lining of our blood vessels, is like the smooth asphalt that ensures easy traffic flow. Wildfire smoke roughens this surface, hindering blood flow and promoting dangerous clots, like roadblocks that bring traffic to a standstill.

Thickening the Plot: Increased Blood Viscosity: Imagine the blood thickening like molasses, making it harder for the heart to pump. This increased viscosity strains the heart, like a truck struggling to haul a heavy load uphill.

The Cardiovascular Casualties: A Grim Toll

The consequences of this smoke-induced chaos are devastating:

Heart Attacks: The smoke triggers plaque rupture in the coronary arteries, leading to heart attacks, like a sudden road closure cutting off vital supplies.
Strokes: Whether it's a blockage or a rupture, strokes are like catastrophic accidents on the brain's highway, leaving lasting damage.
Arrhythmias: The heart's rhythm falters, like a car sputtering and stalling, increasing the risk of sudden cardiac arrest, a fatal crash.
Heart Failure: The heart, weakened and overworked, struggles to keep up, like an engine failing under constant strain.

Vulnerable Populations: Caught in the Crossfire

The smoke doesn't discriminate, but some are more susceptible to its toxic effects:

The Elderly: Their aging cardiovascular systems are like vintage cars, more prone to breakdowns.
Those with Pre-existing Conditions: People with heart disease or high blood pressure are like drivers with prior traffic violations, at higher risk of another offense.
Children: Their developing lungs and hearts are like new roads under construction, more vulnerable to damage.

Pregnant Women: The smoke threatens both mother and child, like a hazardous spill endangering passengers and cargo.

Firefighters and First Responders: They are the front-line workers, like traffic officers exposed to the highest risk zones.

Case Studies: Smoke Signals from the Front Lines

Recent studies paint a grim picture:

California Wildfires: A surge in heart attacks, strokes, and arrhythmias followed the 2018 wildfires, like a spike in accident rates after a major highway closure.

Washington Wildfire Smoke: Emergency rooms overflowed with heart-related cases on smoky days, like a traffic jam of ambulances heading to the hospital.

Montana Wildfire Smoke: Heart rate variability, a measure of the heart's adaptability, plummeted under smoke exposure, like a car losing control on a slippery road.

Protecting Ourselves: Navigating the Smoke-Filled Road

We can't control the wildfires, but we can take steps to protect ourselves:

Stay Informed: Monitor air quality reports, like checking traffic updates before a journey.

Limit Outdoor Activities: Avoid strenuous activities during smoky days, like postponing a road trip during a blizzard.

Filter the Air: Use air purifiers and masks, like equipping our vehicles with air filters and seatbelts.

Seek Medical Attention: Don't ignore warning signs, like pulling over when the car starts making strange noises.

Advocate for Clean Air: Support policies that reduce air pollution, like investing in better roads and safer vehicles.

The Road Ahead: Charting a Course Through the Smoke

The threat of wildfire smoke is a stark reminder of our changing climate. We need more research to understand the long-term impacts and develop better protective measures. But most importantly, we need to act on climate change, to prevent the dragon from breathing fire in the first place. Only then can we ensure a future where our hearts beat strong and healthy, free from the threat of wildfire smoke.

The air crackles with a strange, metallic tang. It's not the scent of pine needles and damp earth you'd expect from a forest, but something acrid, something that claws at the back of your throat. This isn't just smoke; it's the breath of a monster, a wildfire that has devoured homes, landscapes, and lives. But the flames leave more than just charred remains in their wake. They sear invisible wounds into the souls of those who witness their fury, wounds that fester long after the embers have cooled.

Imagine a child, eyes wide with terror, watching the familiar world turn into an inferno. The smell of smoke becomes a trigger, a constant reminder of the day their world shattered. Or picture an elderly woman, forced to flee her home, the life she built reduced to ashes. The loss is more than material; it's the loss of memories, of roots, of a sense of belonging. These are the invisible scars left by wildfires, the psychological toll that often goes unseen.

Wildfire smoke isn't just a physical irritant; it's a mind-altering cocktail of toxins. Studies are revealing a chilling link between smoke exposure and a surge in anxiety, depression, and even PTSD. The constant fear, the disruption of sleep, the haunting images of destruction – they all take their toll.

And it's not just the immediate aftermath. Months, even years later, the trauma can linger. A sudden scent, a news report, a shift in the wind – any of these can rip open old wounds, plunging survivors back into the heart of the inferno.

Who are the most vulnerable? The children, their young minds struggling to comprehend the chaos. The elderly, already facing health challenges, now grappling with loss and displacement. Pregnant women, their unborn children exposed to the insidious toxins. Those with existing mental health conditions, their fragile equilibrium shattered. And let's not forget the marginalized communities, often hit hardest by these disasters, their resources stretched thin, their voices unheard.

We need to do more than just put out the fires. We need to heal the invisible wounds. This means:

   Early intervention: Providing mental health support in the immediate aftermath of a wildfire, offering a safe space to process trauma and grief.
   Long-term care: Recognizing that the psychological impacts can be enduring, and ensuring access to ongoing therapy, support groups, and other resources.
   Community building: Fostering resilience by strengthening community bonds, creating spaces for shared healing, and empowering survivors to rebuild their lives.
   Public awareness: Breaking the stigma around mental health, educating communities about the invisible wounds of wildfire, and encouraging people to seek help.

The flames may subside, but the scars remain. It's time to acknowledge the mental health crisis hidden in the smoke, to offer compassion and support to those who have lost so much. Only then can we truly begin to heal, to rise from the ashes, and to build a more resilient future.

Protecting Public Health: Developing Strategies for Mitigating the Long-Term Health Risks of Wildfire Smoke

Wildfire smoke presents a significant and growing threat to public health, particularly as climate change exacerbates the frequency and intensity of wildfires. The health impacts of wildfire smoke extend far beyond the immediate aftermath of a fire, with long-term consequences for respiratory, cardiovascular, and overall health. Therefore, it is crucial to develop comprehensive public health interventions and policy recommendations to mitigate these risks. This section will focus on three key areas:

Reducing Smoke Exposure: Strategies to minimize individual and community exposure to wildfire smoke.

Improving Air Quality Monitoring: Enhancing monitoring systems to provide timely and accurate information about smoke levels.

Providing Long-Term Health Support: Establishing resources and programs to address the ongoing health needs of individuals affected by wildfire smoke.

Reducing Smoke Exposure

Reducing exposure to wildfire smoke is the first line of defense in protecting public health. This can be achieved through a combination of individual actions, community-level interventions, and broader policy changes.

Individual Actions:

Stay Informed: Utilize air quality monitoring resources (discussed further below) to stay updated on current and forecasted smoke conditions. Reliable sources include:

    U.S. Environmental Protection Agency (EPA) AirNow: Provides real-time air quality data and forecasts across the United States. (www.airnow.gov)

    PurpleAir: A network of low-cost sensors providing hyperlocal air quality data. (www.purpleair.com)

    State and local air quality agencies: Many states and localities have their own air quality monitoring and alert systems.

Limit Outdoor Activities: When smoke levels are elevated, minimize outdoor activities, especially strenuous exercise. Children, older adults, and those with pre-existing health conditions should be particularly cautious.

Create a Clean Air Room: Identify a room in your home that can be sealed off from outside air. Use a portable air cleaner with a HEPA filter to further improve air quality in this space.

Wear an N95 Respirator: When outdoors in smoky conditions, wear a properly fitted N95 respirator. Cloth masks and surgical masks do not effectively filter out the fine particles in wildfire smoke. Resources on proper respirator use and fit can be found on the CDC website (www.cdc.gov).

Community-Level Interventions:

Clean Air Centers: Establish community centers, libraries, and other public spaces as designated clean air centers during smoke events. These centers should have adequate ventilation and filtration systems to provide a safe haven for those without access to clean air in their homes.

Public Awareness Campaigns: Conduct public education campaigns to raise awareness about the health risks of wildfire smoke and provide guidance on protective measures. Target vulnerable populations, such as schools, senior centers, and communities with limited access to healthcare.

Smoke-Ready Communities: Develop community-wide preparedness plans that include strategies for reducing smoke exposure, such as:

Building codes: Incorporate smoke-resistant features into building codes for new construction and renovations.

Urban forestry: Strategically plant trees and vegetation to create windbreaks and filter smoke.

Transportation planning: Reduce traffic congestion during smoke events to minimize vehicle emissions, which can exacerbate air pollution.

Policy Recommendations:

Strengthen Air Quality Standards: The EPA is currently reviewing the National Ambient Air Quality Standards (NAAQS) for particulate matter. Advocate for stricter standards that reflect the latest scientific evidence on the health impacts of wildfire smoke.

Wildfire Prevention and Management: Invest in proactive wildfire prevention and management strategies, such as:

Forest thinning and prescribed burns: Reduce fuel loads in forests to minimize the intensity and spread of wildfires.

Community wildfire protection plans: Develop and implement plans to reduce wildfire risk in the wildland-urban interface.

Support for Vulnerable Populations: Provide targeted support for vulnerable populations disproportionately affected by wildfire smoke, such as:

Low-income communities: Offer financial assistance for air purifiers and other protective measures.

Indigenous communities: Address the unique challenges faced by tribal communities impacted by wildfires.

Individuals with pre-existing health conditions: Ensure access to healthcare and resources to manage their conditions during smoke events.

Improving Air Quality Monitoring

Accurate and timely air quality monitoring is essential for informing public health interventions and protecting communities from wildfire smoke. Advancements in technology and data analysis offer opportunities to enhance monitoring systems and provide more localized and actionable information.

Technological Advancements:

Low-Cost Sensors: The proliferation of low-cost sensors, such as those used in the PurpleAir network, has enabled widespread monitoring of air quality at the neighborhood level. These sensors provide real-time data that can be used to identify hotspots and inform individual decision-making.

Satellite Imagery: Satellite imagery can be used to track wildfire smoke plumes and predict their movement. This information can be integrated with ground-based monitoring data to provide a more comprehensive picture of air quality conditions.

Artificial Intelligence (AI): AI and machine learning algorithms can be used to analyze large datasets of air quality data and identify patterns and trends. This can help to improve forecasting accuracy and provide early warnings of smoke events.

Community Resilience Programs: Build community resilience to wildfire smoke through:

Community education and outreach: Provide information and resources on wildfire smoke and its health impacts.

Social support networks: Connect individuals and families affected by wildfire smoke with support groups and community resources.

Emergency preparedness planning: Help communities develop plans to protect vulnerable populations during wildfire smoke events.

Policy Recommendations:

Expand Health Insurance Coverage: Ensure that all individuals have access to affordable health insurance that covers the costs of wildfire smoke-related healthcare.

Invest in Research: Fund research to further investigate the long-term health effects of wildfire smoke and develop effective interventions.

Address Health Disparities: Prioritize resources and support for communities disproportionately affected by wildfire smoke, including low-income communities, communities of color, and tribal communities.

Case Studies:

The California Wildfire Smoke Study (CWSS): This ongoing study is tracking the health impacts of wildfire smoke on California residents. Preliminary findings indicate increased rates of respiratory and cardiovascular hospitalizations following wildfire smoke exposure. The CWSS is providing valuable data to inform public health interventions and policy recommendations.

The Oregon Smoke Intervention Study (OSIS): This study is evaluating the effectiveness of different interventions to reduce smoke exposure in vulnerable populations.

Interventions being tested include the use of portable air cleaners, clean air centers, and public education campaigns. The OSIS will provide evidence-based guidance for community-level interventions.

The Wildfire Smoke and Children's Health Study (WSCHS): This study is investigating the long-term respiratory health effects of wildfire smoke exposure in children. The WSCHS is following a cohort of children exposed to wildfire smoke to assess their lung function, respiratory symptoms, and overall health over time. The findings of this study will inform public health strategies to protect children from the harmful effects of wildfire smoke.

Wildfire's Wake: Assessing the Ecological Impacts on California's Biodiversity

The 2025 Wildfires: A Scar on the Face of Nature

Imagine our planet as a living tapestry, woven with intricate threads of ecosystems, each supporting a vibrant array of life. Now, picture ruthless flames tearing through this tapestry, leaving behind a patchwork of charred remnants and fragmented habitats. This is the grim reality of 2025, a year marked by unprecedented wildfires that have ravaged landscapes across the globe, from the lush Amazon rainforest to the sun-baked Australian bush.

These fires, fueled by a dangerous cocktail of climate change and human activities, are not merely natural events. They are a stark warning, a blazing testament to our planet's precarious state. The consequences are devastating: habitat loss and fragmentation, two insidious forces that are silently pushing countless species towards the brink.

Remote Sensing: Our Eyes in the Sky

In the aftermath of these fiery infernos, we turn to technology to assess the damage. Satellites, like watchful guardians, orbit the Earth, capturing images of the scarred landscapes below. These images, processed through the lens of remote sensing, reveal the true extent of the devastation.

Think of spectral analysis as a digital fingerprint, allowing us to distinguish between healthy and burned vegetation, while change detection acts as a time machine, comparing before-and-after images to highlight the areas ravaged by fire. Thermal imaging, on the other hand, provides a real-time view of the inferno, tracking the fire's relentless advance.

Field Surveys: Boots on the Ground

While remote sensing paints a broad picture, it is on the ground, amidst the ashes and the skeletal remains of trees, that the true impact of the fires is felt. Field surveys, conducted by dedicated scientists and researchers, provide the crucial ground-truthing, validating the satellite data and delving deeper into the ecological consequences.

Imagine these researchers traversing the scorched landscapes, meticulously documenting the loss of critical habitats, assessing the quality of the remaining fragments, and monitoring the struggling wildlife populations. Their findings paint a grim picture: animals losing their homes and food sources, forced into ever-shrinking territories, their very survival hanging in the balance.

Case Studies: A World Ablaze

The Amazon, the "lungs of the planet," choked by smoke and flames, its iconic biodiversity under siege. Australia, its unique wildlife decimated by raging bushfires, the haunting cries of koalas echoing through the charred eucalyptus forests. California, its majestic landscapes transformed into fiery infernos, pushing species like the California condor closer to the precipice of extinction.

These are not just isolated incidents; they are interconnected threads in a global tapestry of destruction. The 2025 wildfires are a wake-up call, a stark reminder that we are all inextricably linked to the fate of our planet.

The Path Forward: A Call to Action

The scars left by the 2025 wildfires will take years, if not decades, to heal. But amidst the ashes, there is hope. By harnessing the power of remote sensing and field surveys, we can gain a deeper understanding of the ecological damage, inform conservation efforts, and guide habitat restoration initiatives.

However, the ultimate solution lies in addressing the root causes of these fires: climate change and unsustainable human activities. It is a call to action, a plea for global cooperation to protect our planet's precious biodiversity before it is too late. The time to act is now, before the flames of destruction consume the very fabric of life on Earth.

A Fiery Trial: How Wildfires Test Wildlife and Reshape Ecosystems

Imagine a world where flames dance across the landscape, leaving a trail of destruction in their wake. This is the reality for countless animals caught in the path of increasingly frequent and intense wildfires. While fire is a natural part of many ecosystems, the blazes we're seeing today are often supercharged by climate change and human actions, pushing wildlife to the brink.

The Immediate Toll: A Dance with Death

When fire erupts, it's a race for survival. Some animals, blessed with speed or cunning, manage to escape the inferno. Others, less fortunate, become casualties of the flames. Small creatures like rodents and reptiles are especially vulnerable, their homes and lives consumed in an instant. Even larger animals can find themselves trapped, their strength no match for the fire's relentless advance.

But the flames aren't the only danger. Smoke, a suffocating blanket of toxins, fills the air, making each breath a struggle. Animals with sensitive lungs, the young, and the old, are particularly susceptible. Smoke can weaken their defenses, leaving them vulnerable to disease and a slow decline.

Counting the Fallen: A Grim Task

Researchers venture into the charred landscapes, trying to piece together the puzzle of loss. It's a difficult job, like finding needles in a haystack that's been burned to ash. They count carcasses, track survivors, and set up cameras to capture glimpses of life returning. Each piece of data helps paint a picture of the fire's impact, but the true toll may forever remain a mystery.

Beyond the Flames: A Landscape Transformed

The fire may pass, but its legacy lingers. Forests become grasslands, familiar landmarks vanish, and the resources animals depend on disappear. It's like their world has been turned upside down. Some adapt, searching for new territories, while others struggle to survive in a diminished habitat.

Ripples in the Web: The Ecosystem's Unraveling

The loss of even a single species can send shockwaves through the ecosystem. Predators may feast on fire-killed carcasses, only to face starvation later when prey becomes scarce. Prey animals, relieved of their predators, may overgraze the land, hindering its recovery. It's a delicate balance, easily disrupted by the chaos of fire.

Lessons from the Ashes: Stories of Resilience and Loss

The 2020 Australian bushfires, a fiery apocalypse, decimated wildlife populations, leaving behind a scarred continent. Yellowstone National Park, once ravaged by fire, has shown the power of nature to heal and regenerate. California's frequent wildfires serve as a stark reminder of the challenges we face in protecting our wild neighbors.

A Call to Action: Guardians of the Flame

Wildfires are a force of nature, but we have a role to play in shaping their impact. By understanding how fire affects wildlife, we can make informed decisions about land management, conservation, and climate action. It's a responsibility we can't ignore, for the sake of the animals who share our planet and the ecosystems that sustain us all.

Embracing the Inferno: A Rebirth in the Wild

Imagine a wildfire sweeping through a forest, leaving a trail of destruction in its wake. It's easy to see this as an unmitigated disaster, but what if we told you that this fiery chaos is often the prelude to an extraordinary comeback? Like the mythical phoenix rising from its ashes, nature has an incredible ability to heal and regenerate after a fire. Let's delve into this captivating world of post-fire recovery, where life finds a way to flourish amidst the charred remains.

Nature's Grand Recovery Plan

Fire isn't just about destruction; it's a reset button for ecosystems. Think of it as nature's way of hitting "refresh." After the flames subside, a fascinating chain reaction begins, leading to a revitalized landscape.

1. The First Responders

In the immediate aftermath, the scene might look bleak. But beneath the surface, a silent revolution is brewing. The fire has released a treasure trove of nutrients from the burned vegetation, enriching the soil. This nutrient boost acts like a wake-up call for dormant seeds, coaxing them to sprout.

Hardy plants, known as "pioneer species," are the first to emerge. These tough survivors, like fireweed with its vibrant pink flowers, are perfectly adapted to thrive in the harsh, sun-drenched conditions. They're the heroes of the early recovery, stabilizing the soil and preventing erosion.

2. A Symphony of Life Returns

As time marches on, the landscape transforms. Shrubs and young trees take root, creating a more complex tapestry of life. This attracts a wider range of animals – birdsong fills the air, small mammals scurry through the undergrowth, and insects buzz with renewed purpose. The ecosystem is regaining its vibrancy.

3. A Resilient Masterpiece

Eventually, a sense of equilibrium returns. A diverse mix of plants and animals, perfectly suited to the environment, creates a thriving community. Towering trees cast their shadows, while a hidden world teems with life beneath the forest floor.

This isn't a static picture, though. Nature is always in flux. Future fires, windstorms, or even insect outbreaks might shake things up again, ensuring that the ecosystem remains dynamic and diverse.

The Factors at Play

The path to recovery isn't always smooth. Several factors influence how quickly and effectively an ecosystem bounces back:

Fire Severity: A quick burn might just clear out the underbrush, while a raging inferno can obliterate everything in its path, making recovery a longer journey.

Pre-Fire Landscape: A forest with fire-adapted species, like those with cones that only release seeds after a fire, will have a head start in the recovery race.

Climate: The right amount of rainfall and sunshine can make all the difference in helping plants and animals re-establish themselves.

Terrain: Steep slopes and rocky soils can make it harder for plants to take root, while fertile valleys offer a more welcoming environment.

Lending Nature a Helping Hand

While nature is incredibly resilient, sometimes it needs a little help from its human friends. Here's how we can assist in the recovery process:

Habitat Restoration: Planting native trees and shrubs can jumpstart the recovery of plant communities and provide much-needed shelter for wildlife.

Bringing Back the Wildlife: In cases where fire has severely impacted animal populations, we can help by reintroducing species or creating habitats that cater to their needs.

Keeping Invaders at Bay: Invasive species can take advantage of the post-fire environment and muscle out native plants. Early detection and control are crucial to protect the recovering ecosystem.

Monitoring the Comeback: Keeping a close eye on the recovering landscape helps us understand what's working and adapt our strategies as needed. Technology like drones and satellite imagery can give us a bird's-eye view of the progress.

Lessons from the Ashes

Yellowstone National Park: The massive fires of 1988 showed us just how resilient nature can be. Yellowstone's forests and wildlife have made a remarkable comeback, proving that fire is a vital part of this ecosystem.
Australian Bushfires: The devastating fires of 2019-2020 highlighted the challenges of recovery in a changing climate. These fires were a wake-up call, emphasizing the need for proactive fire management and conservation efforts.
The Mediterranean: This fire-prone region has a long history of human interaction with fire. Traditional practices like prescribed burning can help reduce the risk of catastrophic wildfires and promote healthy ecosystems.

The Phoenix Effect in Action

The ability of ecosystems to rise from the ashes is a powerful reminder of nature's resilience. By understanding the intricate dance of post-fire recovery and working in harmony with natural processes, we can help ensure that our planet's wild places continue to thrive for generations to come. Let's embrace the phoenix effect and become champions for fire-adapted and resilient landscapes.

The world is ablaze. It's not just a metaphor; it's the stark reality of the Pyrocene, a fiery epoch where wildfires rage with unprecedented ferocity. Forget Bambi and Smokey Bear – we need a new narrative for conservation, one that dances with flames instead of dousing them.

The Human Exodus: Decision-Making and Behavior During Wildfire Evacuations

Wildfire: When the Mind Catches Fire

Imagine standing on the edge of a precipice, the ground crumbling beneath your feet. That's what it feels like to face a wildfire – a terrifying dance between nature's fury and human resilience. But it's not just the flames that threaten us; it's the fire within our own minds. Our perceptions, our fears, our deeply ingrained biases – these can be as destructive as the inferno itself.

This isn't just about dry statistics and evacuation orders. This is about understanding the human heart in the face of chaos. Why do some flee at the first whiff of smoke, while others cling to their homes until the embers lick at their doors? Why do some heed the warnings, while others dismiss them as overblown?

The Mind's Inferno: A Landscape of Perception

We're not robots. We don't process wildfire threats like cold, hard equations. Our past experiences, the whispers of our neighbors, the newsfeeds flashing on our phones – they all paint a subjective picture of risk.

   Ghosts of Fires Past: Imagine a childhood memory: the acrid smell of smoke, the panicked scramble for safety, the haunting glow of a distant inferno. These experiences sear themselves into our souls, shaping how we react to future threats. But for those who haven't witnessed this raw power, the danger can seem abstract, distant, almost unreal.
   The Echo Chamber: In today's hyper-connected world, information spreads like wildfire itself. But who do we trust?

The official alerts? The frantic posts on social media? The neighbor who swears he's seen it all before? This cacophony of voices can either guide us to safety or lead us astray.

The Pull of the Familiar: Our homes are more than just structures; they're anchors in the storm of life. Leaving them feels like abandoning a part of ourselves. This deep-rooted attachment can blind us to danger, whispering promises of safety even as the flames draw near.

Mental Shortcuts: The Double-Edged Sword

Our brains are wired for efficiency. We use mental shortcuts, called heuristics, to navigate the complexities of life. But in the crucible of a wildfire, these shortcuts can become treacherous pitfalls.

The "It Won't Happen to Me" Trap: We tend to underestimate our own vulnerability. "Sure, wildfires are dangerous," we think, "but I'm prepared. I'll be fine." This optimism bias can lull us into a false sense of security, delaying crucial decisions.

The Power of the First Impression: The initial news report, the first conversation with a neighbor – these early impressions can anchor our perception, making it hard to adjust even as the situation changes. If the first message downplays the risk, we might cling to that reassurance, even as the danger escalates.

The Social Contagion: We are social creatures, constantly looking to others for cues. If our neighbors are calm, we're more likely to stay calm. If they're panicking, our own anxiety rises. This social contagion can either amplify our fear or bolster our courage.

Beyond the Individual: The Tapestry of Community

Wildfires don't just threaten individuals; they tear at the fabric of communities. Our collective response – our shared fears, our acts of solidarity, our willingness to heed the warnings – can determine whether we survive or succumb.

The Strength of Shared Norms: In some communities, the norm is to stay and defend. "We'll protect our homes," they declare, "we won't be driven out." This collective defiance can be both inspiring and dangerous, fostering a sense of unity while potentially putting lives at risk.

The Ripple Effect of Trust: Trust in authorities, in community leaders, in each other – this is the bedrock of resilience. When trust erodes, so does our ability to act decisively. Clear, consistent communication from trusted sources is essential to guide us through the smoke and flames.

From Insights to Action: Rewriting the Narrative

Understanding the psychology of wildfire isn't just an academic exercise. It's about empowering individuals and communities to make life-saving decisions.

Speak the Language of Emotion: Dry facts and figures won't always sway hearts and minds. We need to connect with people on an emotional level, acknowledging their fears, validating their concerns, and inspiring them to act.

Tailor the Message: A one-size-fits-all approach won't work. We need to understand the unique needs and perspectives of different communities, crafting messages that resonate with their experiences and values.

Harness the Power of Social Influence: Instead of fighting against social norms, we need to work with them. Identify trusted community leaders, empower them with information, and encourage them to spread the message of preparedness.

The wildfire is a formidable foe, but the human spirit is even stronger. By understanding the fire within, we can learn to coexist with the fire without, building a future where communities not only survive but thrive in the face of this ever-present threat.

The Evacuation Calculus: A Mind-Boggling Mix of Sirens, Selfies, and Sheer Panic

Forget spreadsheets and statistics. Evacuation decision-making is less about cold, hard logic and more like a frantic game of mental Jenga. One wrong move, and your whole world comes crashing down. So, what exactly goes on in that swirling vortex we call the human brain when the alarm bells start ringing? Let's dive in...

1. The Siren Song of Officialdom (Or, Why You Should Probably Listen to That Guy in the Uniform)

Picture this: Your phone buzzes with an ominous alert. It's not your ex sliding back into your DMs, but a message that screams "DANGER!" in all caps. Suddenly, you're face-to-face with the evacuation calculus. Do you trust that stern-faced official on the TV? Is this a drill, or is it the real deal?

See, official warnings are like that friend who always gives the best advice, even if you don't always want to hear it. They're backed by science, data, and people with fancy titles like "Meteorologist" or "Emergency Management Director." But here's the catch: these warnings need to be clearer than a crystal ball and delivered with the urgency of a runaway train.

Think "5-foot floodwaters swallowing your first floor" instead of "potential for coastal flooding." Nobody has time to decipher jargon when a hurricane is knocking at their door. And if those warnings have been wrong in the past? Well, let's just say your trust battery might need a recharge.

2. Media Mayhem: When Disaster Goes Viral

The TV is a swirling vortex of breaking news, the internet explodes with apocalyptic imagery, and your social media feed is a chaotic mix of panicked posts and "stay safe" messages. Welcome to the media circus, where disaster is the main attraction.

News reports can be a double-edged sword. One minute they're calmly explaining evacuation routes, and the next they're showing a terrified family clinging to their roof as floodwaters rise. It's a rollercoaster of emotions that can leave you feeling more confused than a chameleon in a bag of Skittles.

And then there's social media, the ultimate echo chamber. It can be a lifeline for real-time updates and community support, but it's also a breeding ground for misinformation and fearmongering. Remember that time Aunt Mildred shared a fake tsunami warning that sent the whole town into a frenzy? Yeah, we've all been there.

3. The Herd Mentality: When Keeping Up with the Joneses Could Save Your Life

Ever noticed how you suddenly crave pizza when your coworker orders one? That's the herd mentality in action, and it's amplified tenfold during an evacuation. If your neighbors are packing up the car and your best friend is posting Instagram stories from an evacuation shelter, you're going to feel that pressure to conform.

Of course, there's also the opposite effect. If everyone on your street is chilling on their porch with a glass of sweet tea, you might start questioning if this whole evacuation thing is really necessary. After all, nobody wants to be the only one who overreacted, right?

4. The "It Won't Happen to Me" Syndrome: A Dangerous Dose of Denial

We humans are masters of self-deception. We convince ourselves that we're immune to disaster, that we'll be the exception to the rule. This "optimism bias" can be a real pain in the neck when it comes to evacuations.

Think about it: Have you ever ignored a fire alarm, convinced it was just a drill? Or driven through a flooded road, thinking your car could handle it? We all have that little voice in our heads whispering, "It won't happen to me."

But sometimes, reality bites back. And when it does, those who ignored the warnings are often left with a hefty dose of regret and a soggy living room.

5. The Evacuation Obstacle Course: Because Leaving Isn't Always Easy

Imagine this: You're finally ready to evacuate, but your car is out of gas, your elderly dog refuses to leave the house, and you have no idea where to take your collection of exotic houseplants. Suddenly, evacuation feels less like a safety measure and more like an episode of "Survivor."

Financial constraints, lack of transportation, caregiving responsibilities, beloved pets, fear of looting, medical needs... these are just some of the hurdles that can trip people up on their way to safety. It's like trying to escape a burning building while wearing a blindfold and carrying a suitcase full of bowling balls.

The Bottom Line: Evacuation is a Choose-Your-Own-Adventure with Life-or-Death Stakes

Ultimately, the decision to evacuate is a deeply personal one, shaped by a whirlwind of factors that are as unique as the individuals themselves. It's a gamble, a leap of faith, a test of our instincts and resilience.

So, the next time you hear that siren wail or see that ominous alert flash across your screen, remember this: You're not just calculating risk; you're navigating a complex maze of emotions, social pressures, and practical challenges. And sometimes, the bravest decision is simply choosing to leave.

The air crackles with a strange electricity, a mix of fear and adrenaline. The sky, once a familiar blue, is now a canvas of angry orange and swirling black smoke. Sirens wail in the distance, a chilling symphony of impending chaos. It's a scene ripped from a disaster movie, but for the residents caught in the path of a raging wildfire, it's terrifyingly real.

Evacuation isn't a mere suggestion; it's a desperate fight for survival. Imagine a frantic scramble as families pack their lives into vehicles, the agonizing decision of what to leave behind, the fear of being trapped in a fiery inferno.

Roads become choked arteries, a sea of headlights inching forward while flames lick at the horizon. It's a desperate race against time, where every minute feels like an eternity. Some are forced to abandon their vehicles, fleeing on foot, the acrid smell of smoke stinging their eyes and filling their lungs.

For those with livestock, the situation is even more dire. Horses whinny in fear, their eyes wide with panic. Farmers make heartbreaking choices, cutting fences and setting their animals free, praying they'll outrun the flames.

Reaching safety is only half the battle. Evacuation centers overflow, resources stretched thin. Families huddle together, exhausted and uncertain, their lives reduced to a cot and a blanket. The lucky ones find refuge with friends or family, their homes transformed into temporary shelters.

Communication becomes a lifeline. Phones buzz with frantic messages, social media feeds explode with pleas for help and updates on the fire's relentless advance. But misinformation spreads like wildfire itself, adding to the confusion and fear.

In the aftermath, the landscape is scarred, homes reduced to ash and twisted metal. The lucky ones return to sift through the debris, their lives forever altered. The unlucky ones face the agonizing task of rebuilding, their futures uncertain.

This is the harsh reality of wildfire evacuations, a logistical nightmare fraught with challenges. It's a testament to human resilience and the unwavering spirit of community in the face of unimaginable disaster.

      The 2025 fire season was a brutal wake-up call. We saw families separated, homes turned to ash, and lives tragically lost. It forced us to confront a harsh reality: our evacuation strategies weren't good enough. But from the ashes, we rise. We learn, we adapt, we become stronger.

This isn't just about dry statistics and procedures; it's about people, their stories, and their survival.

Targeted Communication: Cutting Through the Noise

Imagine this: flames licking at your heels, smoke choking the air, and you're bombarded with conflicting information. Panic sets in. That's what happened in 2025. We had a symphony of alerts, websites, and social media updates, but it was a dissonant mess. People were confused, and precious time was lost.

We need clarity. We need a single, trusted voice, like a lighthouse cutting through the fog. This could be a dedicated app that provides real-time fire maps, evacuation orders, and shelter locations. Think of it as a digital guardian angel, guiding people to safety.

But it's not just about technology. It's about trust. We need to empower community leaders – the pastors, the teachers, the neighborhood heroes – to be our messengers. They are the voices people know and believe.

And let's not forget those who are often left behind: the elderly, the disabled, those who don't speak English. We need to reach them with tailored messages in their language, through channels they can access.

Phased Evacuations: The Art of Organized Retreat

Evacuations can quickly descend into chaos. Imagine a frantic rush, roads jammed with terrified people, a desperate scramble for safety. That's where phased evacuations come in. It's like a choreographed dance, guiding people out of harm's way in a controlled, strategic manner.

We need to use technology to map out risk zones and prioritize who leaves first. Think of it as a sophisticated chess game, where we anticipate the fire's moves and move our pieces accordingly.

And let's not forget about transportation. We need to work with agencies to create clear evacuation routes, maybe even using contraflow lanes to get people out faster. It's like creating escape arteries for a community under siege.

Community-Based Preparedness: Turning Neighbors into Lifesavers

We can't just rely on top-down solutions. We need to empower communities to take ownership of their safety. Imagine a neighborhood where everyone knows the evacuation plan, where neighbors check on each other, where everyone is prepared. That's the power of community-based preparedness.

We need to encourage people to create "go bags" with essentials, to harden their homes against fire, and to participate in neighborhood watch programs. It's about turning neighbors into lifesavers.

And let's learn from programs like Firewise USA, where communities work together to reduce wildfire risk. It's about shared responsibility, about creating a culture of preparedness.

The Road Ahead: A Call to Action

The 2025 fires were a tragedy, but they also ignited a spark. We can't prevent wildfires, but we can prevent the loss of life. We can build more resilient communities, where people are informed, prepared, and empowered.

This isn't just the job of firefighters and officials. It's a call to action for all of us. Let's work together, learn from the past, and build a safer future for generations to come. Let's turn the ashes of 2025 into the foundation of a more fire-adapted world.

Trial by Fire: Social Media's Role in Disaster Communication and Misinformation

It's like a digital heartbeat in the face of chaos, isn't it? Social media, once just a place for selfies and cat videos, has become our lifeline when wildfires rage. It's a raw, unfiltered window into the inferno, where official updates clash with the shaky videos of ordinary people caught in the maelstrom.

Imagine: flames licking at the sky, a panicked mother live-streaming her escape on Facebook, the comments section a chorus of prayers and advice. On Twitter, hashtags like #Firestorm2025 become beacons of hope, connecting those who have lost everything with those desperate to help.

Nextdoor transforms into a virtual neighborhood watch, where warnings about shifting winds and encroaching flames travel faster than any news bulletin. GoFundMe pages erupt like wildflowers, a digital outpouring of generosity for families left with nothing but the clothes on their backs.

But it's not just about cold hard facts. It's about the human connection. Strangers become allies, sharing tips on how to soothe smoke-stung eyes or where to find the last gas station with fuel. It's about the collective grief, the shared trauma, and the flicker of resilience that glows even in the darkest of times.

Of course, this digital wildfire has its dangers. Rumors spread like wildfire themselves, and the constant barrage of images and information can leave us emotionally drained. But in a world where disaster can strike at any moment, social media is the town crier, the support group, and the rallying cry, all rolled into one.

It's a messy, imperfect tool, but in the face of nature's fury, it's often all we have. And sometimes, that's just enough.

Think of it this way:

Twitter: The frantic, real-time ticker tape of the disaster, where every second counts.
Facebook: The community bulletin board, plastered with pleas for help, offers of shelter, and heartbreaking photos of what's been lost.
Instagram: A visual chronicle of the fire's wrath and the resilience of the human spirit, captured in photos and stories.
Nextdoor: The whispers in the dark, where neighbors become lifelines, sharing hyperlocal intel that could mean the difference between safety and danger.
GoFundMe: The digital bucket brigade, where donations flow like water to quench the thirst for aid.

This isn't just about technology; it's about how we adapt, connect, and survive in an increasingly unpredictable world. It's about the digital threads that bind us together when the flames threaten to tear us apart.

It's true that social media has become a powerful tool for marginalized communities to connect, share information, and organize during disasters. Here's how it helps:

1. Amplifying Voices and Experiences:

Social media allows marginalized communities to share their firsthand experiences and challenges, countering

mainstream narratives and highlighting often overlooked issues.
This can lead to increased awareness and empathy from the wider public, potentially influencing policy changes and resource allocation.

2. Facilitating Mutual Aid and Support:

Social media enables rapid information sharing within communities, helping people find resources, organize support networks, and coordinate aid efforts.
This is especially crucial when official channels are overwhelmed or inaccessible.

3. Advocacy and Mobilization:

Social media platforms can be used to advocate for policy changes, demand accountability from officials, and mobilize communities for collective action.
Hashtags and online campaigns can raise awareness, generate public pressure, and amplify marginalized voices.

4. Bypassing Traditional Media:

Social media allows marginalized communities to bypass traditional media gatekeepers and control their own narratives.
This can be particularly important for communities that have historically been misrepresented or ignored by mainstream media.

5. Building Resilience:

By fostering connections, facilitating information sharing, and empowering communities to take action, social media can contribute to building long-term resilience in the face of disasters.

Examples:

During Hurricane Katrina, social media platforms were used to share information about rescue efforts, locate missing persons, and organize aid distribution.
In the aftermath of the 2010 Haiti earthquake, social media helped connect survivors with aid organizations and mobilize international support.
Following the 2017 Grenfell Tower fire in London, social media was instrumental in raising awareness of the tragedy, organizing support for survivors, and demanding accountability from authorities.

Overall, social media has emerged as a vital tool for marginalized communities during disasters, empowering them to connect, share information, advocate for their needs, and build resilience in the face of adversity.

Remember: While social media can be a powerful tool, it's important to be aware of its limitations and potential downsides. It's crucial to verify information before sharing, be mindful of privacy concerns, and avoid spreading misinformation or hate speech.

The 2025 wildfire season has been one of the most devastating in recent history, with blazes raging across the globe from the Amazon rainforest to the Australian outback and the American West. These natural disasters have been exacerbated by another, less visible, but equally destructive force: misinformation. The rapid spread of false or misleading information on social media platforms has hindered evacuation efforts, hampered firefighting operations, and eroded public trust in vital institutions.

This subtopic delves into the wildfire of falsehoods that accompanied the 2025 wildfires, analyzing its origins, dissecting its impact, and exploring strategies to counter its spread.

The Anatomy of Misinformation During the 2025 Wildfires

Misinformation during the 2025 wildfire season manifested in various forms, each with its unique characteristics and consequences:

   False Evacuation Orders and Routes:
      Inaccurate evacuation orders, often spread through social media posts or doctored images, led to confusion and chaos, with residents either evacuating unnecessarily or remaining in danger zones. False information about evacuation routes further complicated matters, leading people into hazardous areas or causing traffic congestion that hindered emergency responders.
      Example: In California, a viral tweet falsely claimed that Highway 101 was closed due to a wildfire, causing a mass exodus of residents onto alternative routes, which quickly became gridlocked. This delayed the evacuation of those in immediate danger and hampered the arrival of firefighting crews.

   Exaggerated or Fabricated Fire Maps and Severity Reports:
      Manipulated maps or exaggerated reports about the size and intensity of wildfires created unnecessary panic and distrust in official sources. Some posts even falsely claimed that entire towns had been destroyed, leading to emotional distress and hindering recovery efforts.
      Example: A manipulated satellite image shared on Instagram showed a wildfire in Oregon as being significantly larger than it actually was, causing

widespread fear and prompting residents far from the actual fire perimeter to evacuate.

Conspiracy Theories about the Origins of the Fires:
Conspiracy theories, often fueled by political or ideological agendas, attributed the wildfires to various nefarious actors, including government agencies, environmental groups, or foreign powers. These theories diverted attention from the real causes of the fires, such as climate change and human negligence, and sowed discord within communities.

Example: A widely shared YouTube video claimed that the wildfires in Australia were deliberately started by the government to clear land for development, despite clear evidence linking the fires to prolonged drought and record-breaking temperatures.

Misinformation about Fire Safety and Prevention:
False or misleading information about fire safety practices, such as ineffective home protection measures or dangerous evacuation techniques, put lives and property at risk.

Example: A popular TikTok video claimed that soaking towels in vinegar and placing them around windows would prevent a house from catching fire, a practice that has no scientific basis and could provide a false sense of security.

Disinformation Campaigns by Malicious Actors:
Organized disinformation campaigns, often originating from foreign governments or extremist groups, aimed to exploit the wildfires to spread fear, sow discord, and undermine public trust in authorities.

Example: A coordinated network of Twitter bots spread false information about the ineffectiveness of firefighting efforts in Spain, aiming to create panic and discredit the government's response.

The Impact of Misinformation on Public Perception, Evacuation Decisions, and Response Efforts

The wildfire of falsehoods had a profound impact on various aspects of the 2025 wildfire crisis:

Public Perception and Trust:
Erosion of Trust in Authorities: Misinformation eroded public trust in government agencies, firefighting organizations, and scientific experts, leading to skepticism about official warnings and recommendations.
Increased Fear and Anxiety: The constant barrage of false and alarming information on social media amplified fear and anxiety among the public, making it difficult to assess risks rationally and make informed decisions.
Polarization and Social Division: Conspiracy theories and disinformation campaigns fueled polarization and social division, hindering community cooperation and collective action in the face of the crisis.

Evacuation Decisions:
Delayed or Unnecessary Evacuations: False evacuation orders or inaccurate information about fire threats led to delayed or unnecessary evacuations, putting people at risk and straining resources.
Confusion and Panic: Conflicting information and rumors created confusion and panic among residents, making it difficult to navigate evacuation routes and find safe shelter.
Resistance to Evacuation Orders: Distrust in authorities and misinformation about the severity of the fires led some residents to ignore legitimate evacuation orders, putting themselves and first responders in danger.

Response Efforts:
Hindered Firefighting Operations: False information about fire locations or road closures hampered firefighting operations, delaying the deployment of resources and putting firefighters at risk.
Strained Resources: Unnecessary evacuations and traffic congestion caused by misinformation strained emergency resources, diverting them from critical areas and delaying assistance to those in genuine need.
Misallocation of Aid and Support: Exaggerated or fabricated damage reports led to the misallocation of aid and support, with resources being sent to areas that were not as severely affected while neglecting those in dire need.

Case Study: The California Wildfires of 2025

The devastating wildfires that ravaged California in 2025 provide a stark illustration of the impact of misinformation. A combination of factors, including prolonged drought, strong winds, and human negligence, fueled the fires, but the spread of false information on social media significantly exacerbated the crisis.

False Evacuation Orders: In several instances, false evacuation orders circulated on social media, leading to chaos and confusion. In one case, a doctored image of an official evacuation order caused residents of a small town to flee towards a wildfire, resulting in several injuries and fatalities.
Exaggerated Fire Maps: Manipulated satellite images and exaggerated reports about the size of the fires created widespread panic, prompting unnecessary evacuations and straining resources.
Conspiracy Theories: Conspiracy theories blaming the fires on various groups, including environmentalists and government agencies, circulated widely on social media,

diverting attention from the real causes of the fires and hindering efforts to address them.

The impact of misinformation in California was significant:

Delayed Evacuations: False information about evacuation routes and the severity of the fires led to delayed evacuations, resulting in increased casualties and property damage.
Strained Resources: Unnecessary evacuations and traffic congestion caused by misinformation strained emergency resources, delaying the deployment of firefighters and medical personnel to critical areas.
Erosion of Public Trust: The spread of false information eroded public trust in authorities, leading to skepticism about official warnings and recommendations.

Countering the Wildfire of Falsehoods: Strategies and Solutions

Combating the spread of misinformation during wildfires requires a multi-faceted approach involving various stakeholders:

Social Media Platforms:
Enhanced Content Moderation: Social media platforms need to invest in more robust content moderation systems to identify and remove false or misleading information about wildfires quickly. This includes using artificial intelligence and machine learning to detect and flag potentially harmful content.
Collaboration with Fact-Checkers: Partnering with independent fact-checking organizations to verify the accuracy of information shared on their platforms.
Promoting Authoritative Sources: Prioritizing and amplifying content from trusted sources, such as

government agencies, firefighting organizations, and scientific experts.

User Education: Educating users about how to identify misinformation and providing resources for verifying information before sharing it.

Government Agencies and Emergency Responders:

Proactive Communication: Proactively communicating accurate and timely information about wildfires through official channels, such as websites, social media accounts, and press releases.

Counter-Messaging Campaigns: Developing and disseminating counter-messaging campaigns to debunk false information and conspiracy theories.

Collaboration with Social Media Platforms: Working with social media platforms to quickly identify and remove false information and to amplify official messages.

Community Outreach: Engaging with communities to build trust and provide accurate information about wildfire risks and safety measures.

Individuals:

Critical Thinking: Developing critical thinking skills to evaluate the accuracy of information before sharing it.

Checking Sources: Verifying information by consulting multiple sources, especially official government websites and reputable news organizations.

Reporting Misinformation: Reporting false or misleading information to social media platforms and relevant authorities.

Promoting Media Literacy: Educating oneself and others about media literacy and the dangers of misinformation.

Technology and Innovation:

AI-Powered Misinformation Detection: Developing and deploying artificial intelligence tools to automatically detect and flag misinformation about wildfires.

Blockchain-Based Information Verification: Exploring the use of blockchain technology to create a secure and transparent system for verifying the authenticity of information.

Crowdsourced Fact-Checking: Leveraging the power of crowdsourcing to identify and debunk misinformation.

Conclusion

The wildfire of falsehoods that accompanied the 2025 wildfires highlights the urgent need to address the growing problem of misinformation on social media. By implementing a comprehensive strategy involving social media platforms, government agencies, individuals, and technological innovation, we can counter the spread of false information, protect communities, and support effective wildfire response efforts.

The fight against misinformation is a collective responsibility. By working together, we can ensure that accurate information prevails, empowering individuals to make informed decisions and safeguarding lives and livelihoods in the face of future wildfire crises.

Social Media During Wildfires: A Guide to Responsible Information Sharing

The digital age has transformed how we receive and share information, especially during natural disasters like wildfires. Social media platforms can be powerful tools for communication, community support, and spreading awareness, but they can also contribute to the spread of misinformation and confusion. This guide offers strategies for responsible social media use during wildfires, focusing on verifying information, promoting accurate communication, and combating misinformation.

Understanding the Challenges of Social Media During Wildfires

Social media platforms offer several benefits during wildfires, including real-time updates, community mobilization, and information dissemination. However, they also pose challenges:

   Misinformation and rumors: Unverified information, manipulated images, and deliberate disinformation can spread quickly, causing panic and hindering response efforts.
   Echo chambers and filter bubbles: Social media algorithms can reinforce existing beliefs and limit exposure to diverse perspectives, potentially amplifying misinformation.
   Information overload: The sheer volume of information during a wildfire can overwhelm users, making it difficult to distinguish credible sources from unreliable ones.

Guidelines for Responsible Social Media Use During Wildfires

To navigate these challenges and harness the power of social media for good, individuals, communities, and organizations can adopt the following guidelines:

   Verify Information Before Sharing:
      Check the source: Look for information from official sources like government agencies, reputable news organizations, and verified experts.
      Cross-reference: Compare information from multiple sources to ensure consistency and accuracy.

Be wary of sensational content: Extraordinary claims often require extraordinary evidence. Be skeptical of information that seems too shocking or dramatic.

Use fact-checking websites: Websites like Snopes, FactCheck.org, and PolitiFact can help verify the authenticity of information.

Look for visual cues: Be cautious of images or videos that appear manipulated, out of context, or from previous events. Reverse image search can help verify the origin of an image.

Promote Accurate Communication:

Share only verified information: Avoid spreading rumors or unconfirmed reports.

Use clear and concise language: Avoid jargon or technical terms that may confuse people.

Provide context: Explain the source of information and any relevant background.

Be mindful of emotional language: Avoid using inflammatory language or fearmongering.

Correct misinformation: If you see misinformation, politely point out the inaccuracy and provide a link to a credible source.

Combat Misinformation:

Report misinformation: Most social media platforms have mechanisms for reporting false or misleading content.

Block and mute sources of misinformation: Limit your exposure to accounts that consistently spread false information.

Engage in constructive dialogue: If you encounter someone spreading misinformation, try to engage in a respectful conversation and provide them with accurate information.

Support media literacy initiatives: Promote education and awareness about how to identify and combat misinformation.

Use Social Media for Positive Impact:
Share official updates and safety guidelines: Help disseminate critical information from trusted sources.
Offer support and assistance: Use social media to connect with those affected by the wildfire and offer help.
Coordinate relief efforts: Organize donation drives, volunteer groups, and other support initiatives.
Document the event responsibly: Share firsthand accounts, images, and videos that provide valuable information while respecting privacy and safety.

Best Practices for Specific Platforms

Twitter:
Use relevant hashtags to ensure your information reaches the right audience.
Retweet verified information from official sources and trusted experts.
Use Twitter Lists to filter out noise and focus on reliable information.
Facebook:
Join local community groups to connect with people in your area.
Use Facebook Safety Check to mark yourself safe and check on the safety of others.
Follow official pages of government agencies and emergency services.
Instagram:
Use Instagram Stories to share real-time updates and information.
Use location tags to help people find information about specific areas.

Follow verified accounts of government agencies, news organizations, and experts.

Case Studies

The Camp Fire (2018) and the Australian Bushfires (2019-2020) highlighted the challenges of misinformation on social media and the power of social media for community mobilization and support. These case studies underscore the importance of responsible social media use during wildfire events.

Conclusion

By following these guidelines and best practices, individuals, communities, and organizations can harness the power of social media to promote accurate communication, combat misinformation, and support those affected by wildfires. Remember, verifying information, promoting accurate communication, and combating misinformation are crucial steps in navigating the digital landscape responsibly during wildfire events. By working together, we can build more resilient communities and protect lives and property during times of crisis.

The Retreat Dilemma: Ethical and Practical Considerations of Managed Relocation

Imagine a wildfire sweeping through a landscape, leaving a trail of devastation in its wake. Homes reduced to ashes, cherished memories turned to smoke, lives forever altered. This is the harsh reality faced by communities in fire-prone regions across the globe. But what if there was a way to step back from the flames, to create a buffer between ourselves and the inferno? This is the essence of managed retreat.

Think of it as a strategic withdrawal, a conscious decision to relocate people and assets away from harm's way. It's not about abandoning our communities, but rather about adapting to a changing world where wildfire risks are escalating.

Managed retreat is a proactive approach, a long-term strategy that recognizes the limits of our ability to control nature. It's about choosing to live in harmony with fire, rather than constantly battling against it.

In the realm of wildfire management, there are several strategies we can employ. Accommodation involves adjusting to the impacts of fire by modifying existing structures or implementing protective measures. Protection aims to prevent or minimize the impact of fire through engineering solutions. Resilience focuses on enhancing the capacity of communities and ecosystems to withstand and recover from fire events.

Managed retreat stands apart from these strategies in its approach to risk management. It's about recognizing that sometimes the best defense is a strategic retreat. It's about choosing to relocate development and infrastructure away from hazard zones, rather than trying to fortify them against an increasingly unpredictable foe.

In fire-prone landscapes, managed retreat can take various forms. It might involve relocating communities away from the wildland-urban interface, where human development intermingles with wildland vegetation. It could entail relocating structures away from high-risk wildlands, areas with dense vegetation, steep slopes, and a history of frequent or severe wildfires. And in the aftermath of a wildfire, managed retreat can guide rebuilding efforts in a way that minimizes future risk.

The benefits of managed retreat are numerous. It can reduce the risk to life and property, enhance ecosystem health, and prove more cost-effective in the long run compared to the repeated costs of firefighting, disaster relief, and rebuilding. Moreover, it can foster a more proactive and adaptive approach to wildfire risk, empowering communities to make informed decisions about their future and build resilience to climate change.

Of course, managed retreat is not without its challenges. Relocating communities can disrupt social networks, displace residents, and impact local economies. Political and legal barriers may arise, and ethical considerations must be addressed through transparent and inclusive decision-making processes.

Despite these challenges, managed retreat offers a long-term solution for safeguarding communities and ecosystems in the face of increasing wildfire threats. By embracing this approach, communities can take control of their future and build a more sustainable and resilient future for generations to come.

Let's explore some real-world examples of managed retreat in action:

Bonny Doon, California: After a series of devastating wildfires, this community implemented a voluntary buyout program to relocate residents from high-risk areas.

Boulder, Colorado: This city has incorporated managed retreat into its wildfire mitigation plan, identifying areas where development should be avoided or relocated.

Australia: Following the devastating Black Summer bushfires of 2019-2020, the government has invested in managed retreat programs to relocate communities and infrastructure.

These examples demonstrate the potential of managed retreat to reduce wildfire risk and promote community resilience. By learning from these experiences and embracing a proactive approach, we can create a future where wildfires no longer pose an existential threat to our communities.

In the words of the ancient philosopher Lao Tzu, "The greatest victory is that which requires no battle." Managed retreat embodies this wisdom, offering a path towards a more harmonious coexistence with fire. It's a strategy that recognizes the power of nature, while empowering communities to make informed choices that protect lives, livelihoods, and the landscapes we call home.

spirit of a place in your heart when the place itself is gone? These are the questions that haunt the Isle de Jean Charles, questions that echo through the ages, challenging us to rethink our relationship with the land and with each other.

Houston, Texas: Unequal Waters

In the sprawling metropolis of Houston, the aftermath of Hurricane Harvey exposed a different kind of injustice. Here, the floodwaters didn't discriminate, but the recovery efforts did.

Imagine returning to your flooded home, the stench of mildew heavy in the air, your belongings reduced to soggy debris. Now imagine navigating a bureaucratic maze of aid applications, only to be denied assistance because of a technicality or a lack of resources. This was the reality for many low-income communities and communities of color in Houston, where the promise of "managed retreat" often rang hollow.

"We were left to fend for ourselves," says Rosa, a single mother whose home in a predominantly Hispanic neighborhood was ravaged by the floods. "The buyouts went to the wealthier areas, the ones with the political connections. We were forgotten."

This is the stark reality of environmental injustice, where the burden of climate change falls disproportionately on those least equipped to bear it. Managed retreat, in the absence of equity and inclusivity, can become a tool for further marginalization, deepening existing divides and perpetuating cycles of vulnerability.

Reimagining Retreat: A Tapestry of Voices

These stories, fragments of a larger narrative unfolding across the globe, challenge us to rethink managed retreat not as a simple transaction of land for money, but as a complex human endeavor. It's a call for empathy, for listening to the voices of those on the frontlines of climate change, for understanding the profound connections between people, place, and identity.

It's a call for justice, for ensuring that the burdens of relocation are shared equitably, and that the most vulnerable among us are not left behind. It's a call for creativity, for finding innovative solutions that honor both the needs of individuals and the well-being of communities.

The path forward is not paved with easy answers. It requires a tapestry of voices, a weaving together of diverse perspectives, and a willingness to embrace complexity. It demands that we move beyond the transactional and embrace the transformative, recognizing that managed retreat is not just about moving people, but about reimagining our relationship with the land and with each other in a world irrevocably altered by climate change.

The Great Coastal Exodus: Navigating the Uncharted Waters of Managed Retreat

The salty air whips through Sarah's hair as she stands on the eroding edge of her ancestral home, Isle de Jean Charles, Louisiana. The land, once a vibrant tapestry of marshes and oak trees, is now a skeletal frame, swallowed by the rising tide. "It's like watching a loved one slowly fade away," she whispers, her voice thick with grief and a defiant spark of resilience. Sarah, like many others across the globe, is facing the reality of managed retreat – a bittersweet exodus from a home claimed by the relentless advance of the sea.

This is not just a story of Louisiana. From the sinking villages of Alaska to the crumbling coastlines of the Pacific Islands, communities are being forced to confront a heart-wrenching question: when the land you call home is no longer safe, where do you go?

Managed retreat, a climate adaptation strategy born from necessity, is a complex dance between heartbreak and hope. It's a logistical puzzle, a financial tightrope walk, and a deeply personal journey of loss, resilience, and the struggle to preserve cultural identity in the face of an uncertain future.

The Relocation Equation: A Tapestry of Challenges

Imagine a giant jigsaw puzzle, each piece representing a critical factor in the relocation process. Finding a suitable site is like searching for the elusive corner piece – it needs to fit perfectly with the surrounding landscape, both physically and socially.

    Safety and Resilience: The new location must be a fortress against the rising tides, fierce storms, and encroaching wildfires. Scientists and community members work together, armed with climate models and ancestral knowledge, to decipher the land's future and ensure its safety.
    Environmental Harmony: Relocation shouldn't come at the cost of further environmental damage. Imagine eco-friendly communities, seamlessly integrated with the natural landscape, where green infrastructure flourishes and biodiversity thrives.

Infrastructure and Accessibility: Access to healthcare, education, and employment opportunities are the lifelines of any community. Relocation sites must be well-connected, ensuring that these vital services are within reach.

Community Fabric: A community is more than just bricks and mortar; it's woven from shared stories, traditions, and social bonds. Relocation must prioritize preserving this intricate tapestry, ensuring that cultural centers, gathering spaces, and opportunities for social interaction are at the heart of the new community.

But finding the perfect location is only the first piece of the puzzle. Securing funding is like embarking on a high-stakes treasure hunt, requiring resourcefulness, collaboration, and a touch of good fortune.

The Funding Labyrinth: Navigating the maze of government grants, private investments, and philanthropic contributions can be daunting. Imagine a game board where players strategically move their tokens, unlocking different funding sources and overcoming obstacles like bureaucratic hurdles and competing priorities.

Community Coffers: From bake sales to online crowdfunding campaigns, communities are taking ownership of their future, raising funds to supplement larger sources and fostering a sense of collective agency.

Perhaps the most crucial piece of the puzzle is ensuring an equitable resettlement process – a process that upholds the dignity, rights, and cultural identity of every individual.

Voices Heard: Imagine a council circle where community members, young and old, share their hopes, fears, and visions for the future. Their voices shape every step of the relocation process, ensuring that decisions are made with, not for, the people.

Cultural Continuity: Relocation shouldn't mean erasing cultural heritage. Imagine elders passing down traditional crafts to younger generations in a new community center, keeping the flame of their culture burning bright.

Justice for All: Vulnerable populations, like the elderly, those with disabilities, and low-income families, need extra support during this transition. Equitable resettlement means ensuring that everyone has access to safe housing, healthcare, and opportunities to rebuild their lives.

The Journey Ahead

Managed retreat is not a defeat; it's a testament to human resilience and adaptability. It's a chance to reimagine our relationship with the environment, to build more sustainable and equitable communities, and to write a new chapter in the human story. But this journey requires empathy, innovation, and a collective commitment to ensuring that no one is left behind in the rising tide.

Turning the Tide: How Communities are Taking Charge of Their Climate Future

Imagine a coastal town, the waves lapping a little closer each year, the threat of storms looming larger. Now, picture the people of that town, not as victims, but as the heroes of their own story. They're not waiting for a solution – they're crafting it, together. This is the power of community-driven managed retreat.

Why It Matters: Because Home is More Than Just a Place

Think about your favorite childhood spot – the park where you played, the corner store where you bought candy. Now imagine losing it. That's the reality for communities facing climate threats. Managed retreat isn't just about moving houses; it's about moving lives, memories, and identities.

Traditional approaches often miss this human element, leading to resentment and resistance. But when communities take the lead, something magical happens. They bring their deep-rooted knowledge, their hopes, and their fears to the table. They transform a potential crisis into an opportunity for renewal.

The Building Blocks of Community-Driven Retreat

Open Doors, Open Minds: Imagine a town hall where everyone's voice is heard, from the elders sharing generations of wisdom to the young innovators brimming with ideas. This is what early and continuous engagement looks like. It's about clear information, open dialogue, and shared decision-making.

Truth and Trust: The Foundation of Resilience: In a world of uncertainty, trust is a lifeline. Community-driven retreat thrives on transparency. It means being upfront about the challenges, the resources, and the potential impacts. It's about building bridges of understanding between residents and decision-makers.

The Power of Choice: Charting a New Course: Imagine a community choosing not just where to move, but how to live. They might decide to build a sustainable eco-village, or to revive traditional farming practices. Community-driven retreat honors this right to self-determination. It's about respecting cultural heritage and supporting communities in shaping their own destinies.

Fairness for All: Leaving No One Behind: Managed retreat must be a tide that lifts all boats. It means ensuring that everyone, regardless of their background, has a fair chance at a better future. It's about addressing existing inequalities and providing the support people need to thrive in their new homes.

Growing Stronger Together: Investing in Community Power: Imagine residents equipped with the skills and knowledge to navigate the complexities of relocation. They're learning about community organizing, financial planning, and negotiation. They're becoming the architects of their own resilience.

Real Stories, Real Change

Isle de Jean Charles, Louisiana: The Biloxi-Chitimacha-Choctaw people, facing the relentless erosion of their island home, are leading the way in managed retreat. They're working to create a new community that honors their heritage and traditions while embracing a sustainable future.

Newtok, Alaska: This Yup'ik village, threatened by thawing permafrost and rising seas, is relocating to Mertarvik. They're prioritizing their subsistence lifestyle and cultural traditions, showing the world how to move forward without leaving their past behind.

Fiji: This island nation is taking a community-based approach to relocation, empowering local communities to lead the way. They're demonstrating that managed retreat can be scaled up to a national level while still honoring the unique needs of each community.

The Road Ahead: Challenges and Opportunities
Community-driven managed retreat isn't always easy. It requires funding, consensus-building, and navigating legal hurdles. But the rewards are immense. It's a chance to build stronger, more equitable communities, to preserve cultural heritage, and to foster innovation.

A Call to Action
As climate change reshapes our world, community-driven managed retreat offers a beacon of hope. It's a testament to the resilience of the human spirit, our ability to adapt, and our power to create a better future.

From the Ashes: Protecting and Restoring Cultural Heritage in the Wildfire Era

Cultural Heritage Under Fire: A Call to Protect Our Past

Imagine a wildfire sweeping through an ancient forest, not only consuming trees but also turning irreplaceable archaeological sites and historical structures to ash. This isn't a scene from a dystopian novel; it's a reality that threatens our collective memory.

A Framework for Guardianship

To protect these fragile treasures, we need a comprehensive approach. Think of it as a shield with three layers:

   Exposure: This layer assesses the likelihood of a wildfire striking a site. It's like understanding the enemy's movements. Factors such as location, vegetation, climate, and even a site's history with fire all play a role.
   Sensitivity: This layer delves into the potential damage a wildfire could inflict. It's about knowing the fragility of what we're protecting. Are there exposed artifacts, wooden structures, or irreplaceable paintings? Each element contributes to the site's vulnerability.
   Adaptive Capacity: This layer examines the site's defenses. It's about building resilience. Do firebreaks exist? Are there plans for rapid response? Is the local community involved in safeguarding the site?

Lessons from the Flames

Recent wildfires, like those in California and the devastating fire at Notre Dame Cathedral, serve as stark reminders of the urgency. These events weren't just about lost structures; they were about lost connections to our past.

Empowering Action

This framework isn't just about assessment; it's about empowerment. By understanding a site's vulnerabilities, we can tailor protection strategies. Imagine using advanced technologies like remote sensing to monitor fire risk, or involving Indigenous communities in developing culturally sensitive fire management plans.

Preserving Our Legacy

Protecting cultural heritage from wildfire is a race against time. It's about recognizing that these sites aren't just stones and timbers; they're threads in the tapestry of human history. By embracing a proactive approach, we can ensure that these threads remain vibrant for generations to come.

Let's be the guardians of our past, ensuring that the flames of destruction don't extinguish the embers of our shared heritage.

Preserving Our Past: A Dance with Fire

Imagine a wildfire sweeping across a landscape, its flames licking at the walls of an ancient cliff dwelling, or charring the timbers of a historic homestead. It's a heartbreaking scenario, but one that's becoming increasingly common in our warming world.

Protecting our cultural heritage from the ravages of wildfire isn't just about dousing flames; it's about weaving a tapestry of prevention, resilience, and community action. Think of it as a delicate dance with fire, where we learn to coexist with this powerful force while safeguarding the treasures of our past.

Taming the Flames: Fuel Reduction Strategies

Just like a gardener prunes a tree to keep it healthy, we need to carefully manage the vegetation around our cultural treasures. This means thinning out overgrown forests, clearing away brush and debris, and even using controlled burns to mimic the natural fire cycles that Indigenous communities have practiced for centuries.

Picture a team of experts carefully setting a prescribed burn, the flames dancing across the landscape under their watchful eyes. It might seem counterintuitive, but this controlled fire actually helps prevent larger, more destructive wildfires by reducing the amount of fuel available to burn.

Building for Resilience: Fire-Resistant Construction

Imagine a historic building clad in gleaming metal roofing, its eaves protected by ember-resistant screens. This isn't just a renovation; it's a transformation that makes the structure a fortress against fire.

From choosing fire-resistant building materials like stone and brick to creating defensible spaces around structures, we can make our cultural heritage more resilient to wildfire. It's like giving these treasures a suit of armor, ready to withstand the heat of the battle.

Ready for Anything: Emergency Response Planning

Even with the best prevention measures, wildfires can still happen. That's why we need a plan, a well-rehearsed choreography for safeguarding our cultural resources in times of crisis.

Imagine a team of museum curators carefully packing priceless artifacts, preparing them for evacuation as a wildfire approaches. It's a race against time, but their actions ensure that these treasures will survive to tell their stories another day.

A Shared Responsibility: Community Collaboration

Protecting our cultural heritage from wildfire isn't just the job of experts; it's a shared responsibility that requires the involvement of the entire community. From local residents to fire management agencies, we all have a role to play in this dance with fire.

Picture a community gathering, where archaeologists, fire experts, and Indigenous knowledge keepers share their wisdom and perspectives. Together, they develop a fire management plan that protects both cultural resources and the surrounding ecosystem.

The Future of Preservation: A Tapestry of Hope

As climate change continues to fuel the flames of wildfire, the task of protecting our cultural heritage may seem daunting. But by embracing a holistic approach that combines prevention, resilience, and community action, we can weave a tapestry of hope for the future.

It's a dance that requires careful steps, constant adaptation, and a deep respect for the power of fire. But with every successful preservation effort, we ensure that the legacy of our past will continue to inspire and enlighten generations to come.

The 2025 wildfire season has been one of unprecedented destruction, leaving a trail of devastation across the landscape and impacting numerous cultural heritage sites. These sites, encompassing archaeological sites, historical buildings, and cultural landscapes, hold invaluable records of human history and identity. The fires have not only caused physical damage to these irreplaceable resources but also disrupted ongoing research, conservation efforts, and community connections to the past. This document aims to outline the damage to cultural heritage sites caused by the 2025 wildfires, discuss the challenges and opportunities for post-fire recovery and restoration, and highlight the importance of integrating cultural heritage concerns into wildfire management strategies.

Documenting the Damage

Accurately assessing the damage to cultural heritage sites is a critical first step in the recovery process. This involves:

Rapid assessment surveys: Teams of archaeologists, historians, architects, and conservators are deployed to affected areas to conduct initial damage assessments. These surveys identify sites at risk, document the extent of damage, and prioritize emergency stabilization efforts. For example, in the aftermath of the devastating fires in Maui, Hawaii, teams from the State Historic Preservation Division and the University of Hawai'i conducted rapid assessments of cultural sites, including the historic Lahaina district, to identify damaged structures and archaeological remains.

Remote sensing and aerial surveys: Utilizing technologies such as drones, LiDAR, and satellite imagery, experts can capture high-resolution images and data to assess damage in inaccessible areas, map the extent of burned areas, and identify potential threats to cultural resources, such as erosion and landslides. Following the fires in

Southern California, the California Department of Parks and Recreation used drone technology to assess damage to cultural landscapes and archaeological sites within state parks.

Community engagement: Local communities, Indigenous groups, and traditional knowledge holders possess invaluable information about cultural heritage sites, often undocumented or unknown to researchers. Engaging these communities in the damage assessment process is crucial for identifying and prioritizing sites of significance, understanding the cultural impacts of the fires, and ensuring culturally appropriate recovery efforts. In the wake of the fires in Oregon, the Confederated Tribes of Grand Ronde partnered with state agencies to assess damage to culturally significant sites within their ancestral territory.

Challenges in Post-Fire Recovery and Restoration

The recovery and restoration of cultural heritage sites after wildfires present numerous challenges:

Fragile and unstable remains: Fire can weaken structures, cause materials to deteriorate, and leave sites vulnerable to further damage from weather, erosion, and looting. Archaeological sites, in particular, can be extremely fragile, with fire potentially exposing buried features and artifacts to the elements.

Limited resources and funding: Post-fire recovery efforts often compete for limited resources and funding. Securing adequate financial support for the assessment, stabilization, and restoration of cultural heritage sites can be challenging, especially in the face of widespread damage to infrastructure and private property.

Loss of context and information: Fire can destroy or alter the context of archaeological sites and historical structures, making it difficult to interpret their significance and history. The loss of associated organic materials, such as wood and textiles, can also hinder research and understanding.

Environmental concerns: Wildfires can release hazardous materials, such as asbestos and lead paint, into the environment, posing risks to human health and complicating recovery efforts. Restoration work must consider these environmental concerns and adhere to safety regulations.

Cultural sensitivity and ethical considerations: Working with cultural heritage sites requires sensitivity to cultural values, traditions, and beliefs. Consultation and collaboration with descendant communities, Indigenous groups, and other stakeholders are essential to ensure that recovery efforts are culturally appropriate and respect the spiritual significance of these places.

Opportunities for Post-Fire Recovery and Restoration

Despite the challenges, the aftermath of wildfires also presents opportunities for:

New discoveries and research: Fires can expose previously unknown archaeological features and artifacts, leading to new discoveries and research opportunities. For example, the 2018 Woolsey Fire in California revealed previously undocumented archaeological sites within the Santa Monica Mountains National Recreation Area.

Community engagement and education: Post-fire recovery efforts can provide opportunities to engage local communities in the preservation and interpretation of their cultural heritage. This can include volunteer programs, educational initiatives, and collaborative research projects. In the aftermath of the 2020 CZU Lightning Complex fires in California, local communities participated in archaeological surveys and helped document damage to historical structures.

Improved site management and protection: The recovery process can lead to improved site management practices, including the implementation of fire prevention measures, the development of emergency response plans, and the integration of cultural heritage concerns into land management strategies.

Technological advancements: The use of new technologies, such as 3D scanning and digital documentation, can aid in the assessment, recording, and interpretation of damaged sites. These technologies can also be used to create virtual reconstructions and online exhibits, making cultural heritage accessible to a wider audience.

Resilience and adaptation: The 2025 fires serve as a stark reminder of the vulnerability of cultural heritage to climate change and the increasing frequency and intensity of wildfires. Post-fire recovery efforts can promote resilience and adaptation by incorporating climate-smart practices, such as the use of fire-resistant materials and the creation of defensible space around cultural resources.

Case Studies

Mesa Verde National Park, Colorado: After the 2002 Long Mesa Fire, the National Park Service undertook a multi-year effort to stabilize and restore archaeological sites, including cliff dwellings and other structures. This involved careful documentation, stabilization of damaged walls, and the use of traditional building techniques and materials.

Bandelier National Monument, New Mexico: Following the 2011 Las Conchas Fire, the National Park Service worked with tribal partners to assess damage to ancestral Puebloan sites and develop a comprehensive recovery plan. This included the stabilization of structures, the protection of archaeological resources, and the implementation of fire mitigation measures.

About Author

Dr. Azhar ul Haque Sario is a bestselling author and data scientist with a remarkable record of achievement. This Cambridge alumnus brings a wealth of knowledge to his work, holding an MBA, ACCA (Knowledge Level - FTMS College Malaysia), BBA, and several Google certifications, including specializations in Google Data Analytics, Google Digital Marketing & E-commerce, and Google Project Management.

With ten years of business experience, Azhar combines practical expertise with his impressive academic background to craft insightful books. His prolific writing has resulted in an astounding 2810 published titles, earning him the record for the maximum Kindle editions and paperback books published by an individual author in one year, awarded by Asia Books of Records in 2024. This extraordinary achievement has also led to Azhar being awarded an honorary PhD from World Records University UK, which he will soon receive.
ORCID: https://orcid.org/0009-0004-8629-830X
Azhar.sario@hotmail.co.uk
https://www.linkedin.com/in/azharulhaquesario/